The Homiletical Question

The Homiletical Question

An Introduction to Liturgical Preaching

*For Martin,
Blessings on
your preaching!
B*

William Brosend

Foreword by Thomas G. Long

CASCADE *Books* · Eugene, Oregon

THE HOMILETICAL QUESTION
An Introduction to Liturgical Preaching

Cascade Books
An Imprint of Wipf and Stock Publishers
199 W. 8th Ave., Suite 3
Eugene, OR 97401

www.wipfandstock.com

PAPERBACK ISBN: 978-1-4982-9477-5
HARDCOVER ISBN: 978-1-4982-9479-9
EBOOK ISBN: 978-1-4982-9478-2

Cataloguing-in-Publication data:

Names: Brosend, William.

Title: The homiletical question : an introduction to liturgical preaching / William Brosend.

Description: Eugene, OR: Cascade Books, 2017 | Includes bibliographical references.

Identifiers: ISBN 978-1-4982-9477-5 (paperback) | ISBN 978-1-4982-9479-9 (hardcover) | ISBN 978-1-4982-9478-2 (ebook)

Subjects: LCSH: Preaching. | Liturgics. | Title.

Classification: BV4211.2 .B65 2017 (print) | BV4211 (ebook)

Manufactured in the USA   NOVEMBER 6, 2017

Table of Contents

Foreword

Homiletics, the academic field focused on preaching, is a discipline that hearkens back at least to the time of Augustine's *On Christian Doctrine*. Even though the history of homiletics bears a long, steady, and enduring narrative, the field has not been immune to fashion trends along the way. In just the last century, homiletics has surfed atop a number of new waves rushing toward the shore: neo-orthodoxy's Word of God theology, the sermon as counseling *en masse*, scientific communication theory, the revisioning of the so-called "new hermeneutic" into something called the "new homiletic," the swing toward storytelling, the experiments with dialogue in preaching, the lure of the first-person sermon, the turn to the listener, the idea of the preacher as performer, the fascination with images and video, to name just a few.

These impulses in homiletics are, of course, of uneven weight and value. Some have made substantive contributions to homiletics and, consequently, to the work of preachers, and some are mere baubles and fads. One of the virtues of this new volume in homiletics is that William Brosend has the wisdom to take a deep breath, to step back from the homiletical fray, and to ponder what constitutes the central core of preaching. He does so by posing what he calls "the homiletical question," a powerful query that animates the entirety of this text: *What does the Holy Spirit want the people of God to hear from these texts on this occasion?* This question brings much clarity to the discussion, operating like a magnet, pulling all the disparate iron filings of the preaching event into true alignment.

The first thing one notices about this question is that it begins theologically, not in the sense of conforming to my theology or yours, or even Brosend's, but instead by viewing preaching as theological at its root, as the expression of the desire of the Holy Spirit. What does the Holy Spirit *want?* To begin the homiletical question this way recognizes preaching as not mainly a rhetorical performance of a human agent, but essentially as an act of God.

Nowhere has this conviction been more confidently expressed than in the bold claim of the Second Helvetic Confession of the sixteenth century: "The preaching of the Word of God *is* the Word of God." There you have it: the preaching of the Word *is* the Word, period. It's important to remember that, in the Confession, this is not a mathematical formula. It does excuse sloppy preachers by claiming that the mere act of standing in a pulpit and blathering out whatever is on one's mind under the cover of the "sermon" somehow requires God to swing in on the chandelier and to transform this messy event into the Word of God. Rather the creed works in the other direction, namely that it is God who preaches, it is God who faithfully wills to proclaim the Word, and human beings are graced to be gathered into this divine intention.

This dance between divine intentionality and human cooperation shines a light on a second, perhaps surprising, feature of Brosend's homiletical question: his question doesn't mention the preacher, not explicitly anyway. Why is it that the central question governing this book about preaching leaves the preacher out altogether? It is not because Brosend is uninterested in the preacher; this is, after all, a homiletical textbook aimed at equipping people to become preachers. Rather, the omission comes because Brosend is persuaded that the work and person of the preacher have value only as they are tethered up into the larger arc of divine communication. The Holy Spirit wants people to hear, and it is the Holy Spirit who ultimately provokes that hearing. Deep calls to deep.

Again, the Second Helvetic Confession acknowledges that the Spirit could well have chosen to cut the middle man or middle woman—that is to say, the preacher—out of the preaching equation altogether. But the Spirit, in the mystery of God, has nevertheless chosen human agents to do the speaking. "God," says the Confession, "could indeed, by his Holy Spirit, or by the ministry of an angel, without the ministry of St. Peter, have taught Cornelius in the Acts; but, nevertheless, he refers him to Peter, of whom the angel speaking says, 'He shall tell you what you ought to do.'"

In other words, the preacher is important, but only as she or he serves the primary event, namely the proclamation of the Spirit. It is this truth, the truth the preacher's role is derivative, that infuses this volume with a call to prayer. For Brosend, preaching is a work of the Holy Spirit in which the preacher participates—not by right, personal charisma, or inherent authority—but through discernment and obedience, processes that inevitably begin and end in prayer.

Already we can see how action-filled is Brosend's homiletical question. The verbs are strong. The Holy Spirit *wants*; the people of God *hear*. Preaching is an event (hearing) provoked by a prior event (the Spirit's desiring). It is probably fair to say that the first Christian sermon ever preached, in the sense of faithful followers of Jesus communicating the good news *about* Jesus, was the astonished exclamation of the women returning from the tomb, "The tomb is empty! An angel told us he has been raised!" A sermon is not primarily an op-ed piece of wise reflection on the events of the day or the proclamation of a set of ideas. It is, instead, the announcement of an *event*. In short, preaching is *news*—*good news* that expects an eventful reverberation, in the ears and in the lives of those who hear. This is not to say that sermons don't get around to reflection, to the articulation of ideas, and to pondering what this news might mean in this or that situation, but at the heart of every sermon is the astonished cry, "Something has *happened*. God has acted, and everything has changed!" The eventful character of Brosend's homiletical question underscores the newsworthy quality of preaching.

Finally, Brosend's homiletical question points to the fact that preaching does not occur in the ether. Sermons are grounded in particularities, the particularity of texts and the particularity of contexts. The Holy Spirit desires that the people of God hear a word *from these texts on this occasion*. The writer of Hebrews, a preacher himself, gets at this particularity when he uses the word "today." He says "*Today*, if you hear his voice, do not harden your hearts . . . . But exhort one another, as long as it is called '*today*'" (Heb 3:7–8, 13). The author of Hebrews keeps drumming this word "today" to emphasize that the preaching of the gospel has context. It does not happen in a timeless vacuum but here and now, "today," in the present tense of our real and embodied lives. A particular place, a particular time.

When Brosend's homiletical question probes what the Spirit wants God's people to hear on "this occasion," by "occasion" Brosend means times like the second Sunday in Advent, or the week the stock market crashed, or at the funeral of a saint. But by "this occasion" he also means more than this. He means all that is cinched up in our present circumstances, the "today" that the preacher of Hebrews named.

Edmund Steimle, a gifted teacher of preaching in the middle of the last century, once observed that, as a young preacher, he greatly admired the sermons of a certain famous and respected pulpiteer, a man who had a talent for using arresting images and memorable turns of phrase. But as he read sermon after sermon from this celebrated preacher, Steimle gradually began noticing that most of the sermons could have been preached in any year in almost any century. They could have been preached in 1970, or in 1870. In some essential way, Steimle concluded, they were not gospel sermons, because the gospel is always a word on target, a word for "today," a word to and for the hearers immersed in their very concrete circumstances.

Brosend shrewdly discerns that, for the preacher, giving mind to the particularity of *context* begins by attending to the particularity of *text*. For Brosend, biblical texts are not merely lections, liturgical obligations thrust upon the faithful through the constraints of the lectionary. Rather, they are conversation partners for the preacher. Texts "speak," and therefore they must be listened to carefully and reckoned with responsibly.

So, the ingredients of preaching are all in place, named by the homiletical question: the desire of the Holy Spirit, the hearing of God's people, the biblical texts that engage preachers in provocative conversation, and the specific contexts of the hearers. But these ingredients are not free agents; instead, they are interlocking realities, working together to evoke the event of faithful preaching. Together they form the galaxy that is preaching, and, in this galaxy, the preacher is but one planet circling the sun.

Because Brosend's homiletical question begins with the desire of the Holy Spirit, it gives readers of this volume a place to stand while pondering a mystery that has perennially intrigued homileticians and preachers alike: the surplus often experienced in sermons. By "surplus," I mean to point to the experience of every preacher that much more happens in sermons than preachers plan, control, or understand. The sermon that feels weak to the preacher almost inevitably gets the response from some hearer, "I really needed that." Perhaps the preacher comes to worship with a fever and a throbbing headache, or fresh from a not-quite-finished argument with one's spouse, or wounded and angry over a nasty, unsigned letter received from an anonymous parishioner, and the sermon that day feels like drudgery or like emotional turmoil, frail words barely stammered out. And yet, someone at the door says, "I felt like you were preaching from your heart today!" There are many possible reasons for such experiences, but one reason is surely that the Holy Spirit desires more and speaks more than we know, an abundance beyond the preacher's fragile words. The surplus of preaching.

Homiletician and ethicist Ted A. Smith discovers some of this surplus in what he calls "prodigal narratives," stories that preachers tell to make a point but which are larger than the preacher's point and, therefore, overflow to proclaim larger truths. Smith cites as an example a sermon story told by the nineteenth-century evangelist Charles Finney. Finney was trying to make the point that the Holy Spirit gives the gift of spiritual discernment, so that the faithful can perceive the movement of God in their lives and in the world around them. To make this point, Finney told a story about a woman in New Jersey who discerned in a revival meeting that God was about to send spiritual empowerment to those present, what she called "the latter rain." And, indeed, according to Finney, this "latter rain" did, in fact, fall upon those in the meeting.

Now, Finney was a great advocate for women's education, but, as Smith notes, "he was always cagey about whether he thought women should preach." In the story about the woman in New Jersey, Finney made his intended point, but "prodigal details [leaked] out around the edges." His story spoke more truth than Finney planned or thought. Smith says,

> The woman's faithful preparations indicate that she was running a house church. They suggest that she was the preacher and that God blessed her work. Finney did not mean to tell *that* story. But he did. The Gospel truth of a preaching woman found its way through the seams of a story designed to illustrate another point.[1]

That the homiletical question should yield answers that are beyond the reach of the preacher, answers that manifest preaching as an event of surplus and abundance, answers that point toward the mystery that is the Holy Spirit, answers that take us to our knees in prayer before they take us into the pulpit, would come as no surprise to Brosend. That very mystery, that very abundance, is at the heart of Brosend's theology of preaching, and, therefore, at the heart of this book.

Thomas G. Long
Bandy Emeritus Professor of Preaching
Candler School of Theology
Emory University

1. Smith, "Eschatological Memories of Everyday Life," 41.

Acknowledgments

This book represents what wisdom has been gained in a lifetime of preaching and half a lifetime of teaching. The debt to my listeners and students, especially the Master of Divinity and Doctor of Ministry in Preaching students at the School of Theology, University of the South, is incalculable and unpayable. Along the way many colleagues shared in the explorations and in conversations that gave shape to the Homiletical Question, including Earl Johnson, Ben Witherington III, Barbara Brown Taylor, David Buttrick, Susan Springer, Thomas Long, the late Marcus Borg, Vernon Robbins, Micah Jackson, Timothy Sedgwick, Martin Seeley, Ben Anthony, Amy-Jill Levine, and above all, the late Fred B. Craddock. The manuscript was drafted while on sabbatical from the School of Theology, with assistance from the Conant Fund of the Episcopal Church. To the fund, and to Dean Neil Alexander, many thanks. Lauren Winner, Nora Gallagher, Frank Griswold, and Tom Long read and commented on an earlier draft of the manuscript. Dann Wigner assisted in preparing the manuscript for publication. I owe thanks to B. J. Heyboer for introducing me to Rodney Clapp and the good people at Cascade Books. Permission to quote the two Wendell Berry poems in chapter six was granted by Counterpoint Press. An earlier version of the Introduction was published in the *Sewanee Theological Review*.

Finally, family. Emily has listened to more sermons than any child should endure; Mary Ann has exploded into my life, and they both supported me through recovery, writing, and revisions. This book is dedicated to them with gratitude beyond words.

Soli Deo Gloria
Pentecost, 2017

Introduction – The Homiletical Question

One should not be surprised that the development of a preaching professor has much in common with the development of a preacher. The first time, and often a lot more than the first time, both preacher and professor have no idea what they are doing. They ask one to preach *because* she is going to seminary or a diaconal training program, or discerning whether to go, not waiting until she has taken "Introduction to Preaching." They ask her to teach because they have heard she is a good preacher, not because she has mastered the art and craft of teaching. Like people who cannot give directions to the house they grew up in because they never needed to know the names of the streets, one may have heard thousands of sermons and lectures, but not given much thought to how such things are made.

After a while though, as a preacher and teacher of preaching, one begins to get the hang of it. Or at least to stop panicking when called on for a sermon or lecture. And just as preachers move beyond working one Sunday at a time, teachers grow past trying to stay just one lecture ahead of the class. This growth and experience has its own set of dangers, as both teacher and preacher can become too casual in their approach, or lazy in their preparation. Everyone has heard those lectures and sermons.

Preachers come to focus on a set of core convictions, and learn how to retell cherished and powerful stories with great effectiveness, if sometimes forgetting they have already told this audience that story. Teachers of preaching do the same, refining their pedagogies, reshaping the syllabus, learning assigned readings by heart. This wisdom finds its way into articles and book chapters, occasionally to invitations to give guest lectures at other schools or at conferences.

Finally, the preacher decides to reshape his or her "greatest hits" into a volume for publication—which always turns out to be slimmer than expected. And one day the teacher of preaching becomes convinced that it is time to take the audacious step of writing not just another book, but a

1

book that outlines her or his "method"—the fruits of decades of teaching distilled for the ages. This is that book. The Introduction is devoted to the first sixty minutes of sermon preparation, the first sitting down with the readings on which your sermon will be grounded. Like the chapters to follow it will be in three sections: theory, practice, sermon.

Theory

How does one begin? When one has never or only rarely preached, is still mastering the intricacies of the Revised Common Lectionary Old Testament tracks in the season of Pentecost, or is finally invited to preach sometime other than the First Sunday after Christmas or the Second Sunday of Easter, how does one start? And this being a book about liturgical preaching from one who is surprised and delighted to find himself in the Anglican tradition, is there a distinctively liturgical way to begin, a via media of homiletical preparation that might also speak to other ways of preaching? There is, and it begins with recognizing that there are all sorts of starting places.

One may begin with the Collect for the Day. The *Lectionary Page* and similar websites (www.lectionarypage.net) helpfully place the collect right at the top of the page. Doing this brings the mind and heart to homiletical attention, with the added advantage of getting the preacher outside of her or himself. The preacher may begin there, but it is not recommended. After preaching for a while one realizes that the Collect of the Day fits one liturgical year much more closely than it does the other two, which means the preacher has a two out of three chance of being sent in the wrong direction at the very start of the preparation process.

So perhaps it is better to start with some attention to the liturgical year. What is the season, where are we in that season, and what is coming in the next week or two? This can be a useful practice, but it is not recommended. It is a classic "I-go-to-church-every-Sunday-so-I'll-assume-everyone-who-will-hear-this-sermon-does-too" rookie mistake. It also leads one to preach about "our Lenten journey" to people who are thinking about St. Patrick's Day or "March madness," and to making frequent references to "the Great Fifty Days of Easter" to people who did not make it halfway through Rick Warren's *Forty Days of Purpose* and wonder if the preacher is talking about the sequel.

INTRODUCTION – THE HOMILETICAL QUESTION

The texts. Start with the biblical text! When preaching one is proclaiming the word of God, so of course start with the biblical texts. What could possibly be more obvious? True enough, but nevertheless it is not recommend as the place to start. Which text will one begin with? Old Testament or Gospel? Why not the epistle, or in months with five Sundays, the Psalm? Read them in chronological order? But is that the chronology of the historical events presumed by the text or the chronology of composition? Should one read the epistle before the gospel if it is Galatians, but after if it is Titus? And how does one know whether to read the Psalm before or after the Old Testament lesson? If one always starts with the Old Testament, might that not lead to sermons that too often flirt with supersessionism, even if all one is after is a dramatic and inspiring conclusion?

A good case can be made for starting with current events. What is going on in the world, the community, the parish? Are there wars or rumors of war? Is it Super Bowl Sunday? What about the election? Keeping the ways and worries of the world in view is important, but it is not recommended as the best place to begin sermon preparation. For one thing, in this day news sources are so ubiquitous and personalized that one person has never heard about what was screaming from the headlines of the next person's iPad. And then there is the problem those in the homiletics profession refer to by its technical name, "Saturday." Assuming the preacher will later follow the advice to work further ahead than a few days, how does he or she know what actual current event is going to be on the minds of the listeners when beginning to prepare the sermon? One asks this question, but does not start with it.

If not the Collect for the Day, not the liturgical season, not the biblical texts, not the world around us nor the life of the community, exactly where should one start? That is a very good question, and please do start with a question. But not just any question, because one needs to start with the liturgical season, the biblical texts, and what is happening in the world *and* the life of the community. Not one or the other, all of it, all at once. If preachers ask the same question every time, without fail, they make a good beginning, and a particularly liturgical one, holding possibilities in tension and not surrendering to the premature resolution of, "I think I'll talk about Paul today." Because not only will this question never let the preacher down, it will always keep the preacher honest, and get her off to the right start by asking not "What do I want to preach about?" but:

1. *What does the Holy Spirit want*

2. *the people of God to hear*

3. *from these texts*

4. *on this occasion?*

The homiletical question (HQ) does not start with the preacher—this is among the many debts we owe to the late Dr. Fred Craddock. The task is not to gain a hearing for the preacher, but to preach in such a way that the good news is heard, the kingdom proclaimed. In fact, sometimes the preacher's task is simply to get out of the way. When was the last time someone said, "You know what I love about Christmas Eve? The *homily*."

But there is a more important sense in which the preacher must get out of the way—preachers do not lead, they follow. The Holy Spirit leads. Scripture leads. The liturgy leads. The lives of the listeners lead. This crazy, crazy world, "our island home," leads. The preacher looks around, listening to it all, and senses the connections. Not "makes the connections"—they are there or they are not and no amount of pounding the homiletical square peg will get it to fit into the exegetical round hole. A "for instance" will probably help, and it is best to go with an easy one, Proper 10B. The Gospel is Luke 10:25–37, the parable of the Good Samaritan.

What does the Holy Spirit want . . .

The first part of the HQ seems really presumptuous—what does the Holy Spirit want? As if the preacher knows the mind of God. But how much more presumptuous is this question than considering the faithful, gathered to worship God, and asking, "What do *I* want to talk about?" Important to this approach to the preaching task is understanding how to keep the preacher out of the way of the proclamation. On the surface this can become a nonsense debate about whether the preacher should use the first person singular and how much of "our story" we should share. That issue comes later in the sermon development process. The HQ tries to help preachers keep their "stuff" from getting in the way of gaining a hearing for the good news.

So start with the Holy Spirit. Which means starting with prayer. Not the prayer of, "Dear Jesus, help me write a really good sermon." Instead think of the prayer that either is or is not a part of the fabric of one's being.

The prayer of one's breathing in and breathing out. Blame it on the SATs and other test preparation courses, but for whatever reason if given a task that requires one to use their brains many build a "wall of separation" from their spirits. *Nous v. Pneuma.*

But the preacher is not giving a lecture, or arguing before the Supreme Court; the preacher is proclaiming the good news of God's reign in the midst of a wondrously rich liturgy. Doesn't a shout out to the Spirit of God make some sense? So the prayer is more like, "Hi God, it's me. Remember me? You picked me for this assignment, although I have to tell you, not in a voice loud enough for everyone on the Commission on Ministry to hear very clearly. Anyway, I'm up in a couple of weeks. It's the 'Good Samaritan.' I know. How many sermons have they heard on that one? So since this whole preaching/pastor/priest thing was your idea, and you told this story in the first place, it would be fantastic if we could work together on it. Amen." *What does the Holy Spirit want . . .*

The people of God to hear . . .

The preacher has prayed and is praying. In fact the preacher is not going to stop praying. And in a fundamental way the prayers are not for the preacher, they are for our listeners. Remember them? There is often talk about "the audacity of preaching"—who is the preacher to stand up there and talk about God? What about the "audacity of listening"? Sitting there, waiting, not exactly brimming with anticipation, but with some expectation, really an unspoken longing that the preacher will talk about something the listener cares about, and in a way she or he can understand. Is that not the dictionary illustration of "hope"?

One starts by invoking the Holy Spirit but one always remembers that the preacher is asking the listeners' questions, not just the preacher's, and pray God not just the questions the preacher was taught to ask in seminary. This is not anti-intellectualism, this is Jesus. In *The Preaching of Jesus*, it was argued that one of the qualities that characterized Jesus' teaching and preaching is its dialogical nature. To borrow from Dr. Micah Jackson's unpublished doctoral thesis, it is unfailingly conversational, full of back and forth and "What do you think?" Dialogical preaching is fundamentally liturgical, participatory. Not that both sides of the conversation are always given voice, or that Jesus usually tells people what they want to hear. Ask

Jesus a direct question and the answer is likely to be either another question or a story.

Jesus has a big advantage over other preachers. He's Jesus. So one needs to be intentional about asking the questions the listeners are asking when they hear the texts on Sunday morning. And one needs to acknowledge that the only person within the sound of the sermon who has been thinking about these texts all week is the preacher, in a way the greatest advantage and the biggest challenge—how does one close the gap between having just heard the lesson and having been thinking/praying/studying the texts for a week or more?

By asking, with the help of the Holy Spirit, what the listeners' questions are likely to be. What will interest them in the Gospel? What do they need to know to more fully understand the Old Testament lesson? What in their lives maps the same geography as the psalm? In other words, what is going to have to happen in the sermon for the people of God to hear; not what does the preacher want to say but how does it need to be said so that what the Spirit wants to be heard has a chance?

Learning to do this is one of the few things in ministry that gets easier over time. What makes learning how to ask the listeners' questions easier over the course of one's ministry is not the return of the Propers every three years, it is how much better one knows the people one is preaching with after three years. The preacher does not have to wonder what their questions might be, because they have voiced them in countless ways. One has sat in their homes and sat by their hospital bed and sat in prayer before rising to preside at their mother's funeral. Preachers learn their questions, and they will take precedence over the preacher's own and those of the preacher's teachers. After all, neither professors nor the authors of the commentaries one studies will hear a word of the sermon. Asking the listeners' questions will go a long way toward making it possible that what the Holy Spirit *wants* will be heard. *What does the Holy Spirit want the people of God to hear . . .*

From these texts . . .

What does the Holy Spirit want the people of God to hear from these texts? Yes, there are texts, lots and lots of texts, not all of them biblical. Even when the lectors read too quickly those in liturgical traditions spend an amazing amount of the worship hour listening to texts. Add a sequence hymn, a nice musical setting of the psalm, and the time spent waiting for the torchbearers to get the torches back in the stands and themselves in their seats and fifteen to twenty minutes has been devoted to listening to texts. That is quite an investment. Which is one of the more practical reasons that the HQ expects the preacher to be guided by the biblical texts when discerning what it is the Holy Spirit wants the people of God to hear. There are other reasons—tradition, authority, expedience to note three—but when one has spent all that time listening it is rude (and how un-Christian is that?) to ignore them. Yes, there are times when the texts are far from ideal. In which case the preacher has to work harder, and in no case does the preacher begin the sermon by complaining about the lessons. If one is ever tempted to begin the sermon by saying something like, "These have to be the dullest texts in the lectionary; I wonder what I did wrong to deserve being assigned to preach this week?" or "I have to tell you, I wish I had had more time to prepare for today because these texts are *hard*," remember that soon all will pray, "and lead us not into temptation." Good preachers never yield to the temptation to complain about Scripture because it is always a privilege to proclaim the good news of God's love.

So the HQ shifts its focus to "from these texts." There are three or four, depending on the liturgy, and they are equal claimants on the preacher's initial attention. One would not know it to listen to most preachers most of the time but Jesus somehow managed to proclaim the kingdom of God without once mentioning Matthew, Mark, Luke, or John. So honor all the texts, with prayer and the lives and questions of those one hopes will be listening on Sunday. For instance, what does the Holy Spirit want the people of God to hear from the readings of Proper 10C, the Sunday closest to July 13? These are not unfamiliar texts—Deuteronomy 30 or Amos 7, with the accompanying psalm, the beginning of Colossians, and the parable of the Good Samaritan bracketed by Jesus' conversation with the lawyer. For many preachers the first temptation is to start discounting one text or another— "We agreed to follow NRSV lectionary track two at my parish this summer so I only need to read Amos," or, "I don't think Paul wrote Colossians so I'll just kind of ignore it." And the worst temptation of all, "I know the parable of the Good Samaritan."

No, you don't. Preachers know stuff about the parable of the Good Samaritan. They know what they remember they thought it was about the last time they read or studied it. They may know what scholars like John Dominic Crossan and Brandon Scott and Luise Schottroff think the parable is about. But they do not have any idea what the Holy Spirit might want the people of God to hear about and from the parable of the Good Samaritan this time around until they ask. Honestly and openly ask.

One might start like this, recalling everything one thinks the listeners might know about Samaritans. Does not take long, does it? Then try it this way: what do the listeners need to know about Samaritans before they can appreciate the parable? That depends; the preacher does not know yet because the preacher does not know what the answer to the homiletical question is. One could rush to the library, pull down the Anchor Bible Dictionary or some other reference and read for hours about Samaritans. What happens? The preacher ends up giving a lecture on Samaritans, which might be great but is only rarely what the Holy Spirit has in mind, any more than the Spirit often wants one to carefully explain the critical difference between *hizzeh* and *nabi* in Amos 7 because the preacher had two semesters of Hebrew. It may come up, it may even become important to the sermon, but it is does not start out as important.

One clue when it is time to preach on Proper 10C: everything one needs to know is in Luke, and Deuteronomy tells us so. "Surely, this commandment that I am commanding you today is not too hard for you, nor is it too far away. It is not in heaven . . . . Neither is it beyond the sea . . . . No, the word is very near to you; it is in your mouth and in your heart for you to observe" (Deut 30:12–14).

So it's right there. It can be a lot of things—but on this reading one notices that the Samaritan is described as "traveling." He is going someplace. Later in the story one learns that the Samaritan expects to come back. Usually one does not think of this Samaritan as a person, but as a one-dimensional character who exists solely to be a good example for readers of Scripture. It turns out he has a life, and apparently a job; and that job is not to run around helping people. Helping people, even strangers or foreigners, is just something he takes the time to do while he is living his life. It is not too hard, too far . . . the word is very near us, on our lips and in our hearts, that we may do it. *What does the Holy Spirit want the people of God to hear from these texts . . .*

On this occasion

On this occasion. What occasion? To tell the truth there is not always an occasion except Sunday. Which should be enough. As a rule, yes it is. In fact if one finds that some "occasion" or another regularly trumps the biblical texts, there is a problem. But stuff happens, and it has to be factored into the answer to the question. Recall the second Sunday of September some years ago. September 11, 2011, the "10th anniversary" of 9/11. If one preached that Sunday one remembers the Gospel that day, from Matthew 20, very well—the parable of the "Unforgiving Servant." The Holy Spirit was pretty loud and clear on that one. Other times are also obvious—weddings, funerals, baptisms, feast days—and the texts usually help the preacher along.

But it is much more likely that the occasion comes out of nowhere, or seems completely unrelated to the texts. The Third Sunday of Advent, 2012 was two days after the murder of twenty-six elementary school students and teachers in Newtown, Connecticut. The epistle was Philippians 4, "Rejoice in the Lord always!" And the Gospel was John the Baptist from Luke, "You brood of vipers ... bear fruits worthy of repentance." Preachers everywhere scrambled to revise the sermon crafted for *Gaudete* Sunday just a few days before Christmas. The occasion demanded it.

One final thought about the occasion—it does not always have to be tragic to be included in the sermon. Good things happen in the life of the community: deployed soldiers come home, students graduate, a company in town expands, another one adopts new, "greener" policies and practices, it is your patronal feast day, there was a wedding yesterday and everyone was there. Preachers are mistaken if they think the only "occasions" that should find its way into their sermons are tragic.

Focus

What does the Holy Spirit want the people of God to hear from these texts on this occasion? The HQ has expanded over the years to be more encompassing, and then contracted to be more focused. Focus. Maybe it is because most cameras now do it automatically, but many preachers have trouble focusing. Homiletical ADHD. Preachers love choices, but choices are sometimes also temptations, like whining about the lectionary text. And this: one will not have the luxury of weeks to prepare that one did in seminary.

Many times the tentative answer to the HQ is in multiple parts. Proper 7C has the cherished epiphany to Elijah on Mount Horeb, the exorcism of the "legion" of demons from the Gerasene demoniac in Luke, and the "baptismal formula" from Galatians. It is a biblical feast. Does this work as a preliminary answer to the HQ:

God's love for a hurting world is revealed in the "still, small voices" around us so our task as God's people, one in Christ, is to silence the earthquake of empire, the wind of warfare, and the fire of inequality through our prayer and activism, which we can best do by making banners and joining the protest march down Broad Street next Saturday.

Okay. One cannot disagree with the nobility of the preacher's intent, but it is not focused enough to work as a preliminary answer to the HQ. A preacher might end up here but could not start here. In fact this "answer" to the HQ is both without focus and oozes ideology and agenda, something most preachers do not have to worry about including in the answer to the HQ. What most preachers do have to worry about is keeping ideology and agenda from always taking pride of place in their preparation, in effect determining the answer before really asking the question.

What might the Holy Spirit want the people of God to hear from these texts on this occasion? It may depend where one lives—earthquake, wind, and fire are heard differently in California and Oklahoma than in, say, Green Bay, Wisconsin.

Sometimes a little detail grabs the attention and will not let go. In the Gospel Jesus tells the demoniac to return home. In the Old Testament reading God tells Elijah to return to Damascus. It sounds like some unfinished business, which is also what Paul finds himself dealing with in Galatians. Perhaps the preliminary answer to the HQ for Proper 7C is, "The Holy Spirit wants the people of God to see and feel and hear how God heals and renews for the new challenges and the unfinished business still waiting for us at home."

Could this be too much about the preacher's "stuff," everything that is waiting for her or him at home? Yes, it could be, but it is not as if the preacher's family is the only one with issues. And as the preacher tests out this preliminary answer to the HQ during the sermon development process it may get modified, it may even have to be abandoned. So be it.

Still, remember where one started—with the idea that preachers are after gaining a hearing not for themselves, but for the good news. That takes time, and the sooner one decides on a preliminary answer to the HQ the more time one will have to work on getting that answer heard. This cannot be stressed too much: while there is *one* homiletical question on any given Sunday there are thousands and thousands of faithful answers. Pick one. It will likely be true to people and text and Spirit and occasion. Will it be interesting? Will it be heard? That is up to the preacher, and that is what the rest of this book is about.

Practice

One has by now the homiletical question well in mind: what does the Holy Spirit want the people of God to hear from these texts on this occasion? We have looked at a smattering of texts and imagined how one might begin to answer the HQ. This section looks at a specific set of readings and recreates how the preacher spent the first hour of sermon preparation. The readings are from the Fifth Sunday after Epiphany, Year B, or as it is known to liturgists, "Super Bowl Sunday."

The readings are phenomenal, as is generally true in Epiphany every year.

1. Isaiah 40:21–31. "Have you not known? Have you not heard? . . . those who wait for the LORD shall renew their strength, they shall mount up with wings like eagles, they shall run and not be weary, they shall walk and not faint."

2. Psalm 147, a joyous celebration of God's goodness.

3. 1 Corinthians 9:16–23: "I have become all things to all people, that I might by all means save some."

4. Mark 1:29–39, Jesus heals, exorcises, and "In the morning, while it was still very dark, he got up and went out to a deserted place, and there he prayed."

What does the Holy Spirit want

Just reading these texts is renewing and inspiring. The act of reading itself is a form of prayer. Right away, however, the contrast between frenetic activity (young men falling exhausted, Paul becoming "all things to all people," Jesus healing "all who were sick or possessed") and the quiet renewal of those who wait on the Lord, of Jesus at prayer, seems important. How could the preacher convey the contrast in a sermon in a way that would allow the listeners to *feel* it in the same way the preacher does in praying with these texts?

The people of God to hear

Who are the listeners? As often happens in my calling as a seminary professor this sermon was prepared for a congregation I do not really know, for I
am the guest preacher at a parish outside Baltimore. The parish has a school,
an impressively old (by US standards) cemetery, and has been transformed
from being rural to suburban by the growth of the Washington/Baltimore
area. While there might be one or two farming families, from what I have
been told the typical parishioner works for the federal government or for an
agency or company whose work (defense, biotechnology, national security,
computer software) is funded by the government.

It is safe to assume they are very, very busy. Husband and wife both
work outside the home, children are involved in countless extracurricular
activities, and if they sit together in worship it may be the most time they
spend together as a family all week. What does the Holy Spirit want these
people to hear? Peace?

From these texts

The reading from Isaiah is stirring and comforting. Both the OT lesson
and psalm praise God as creator, but even more so praise God as re-creator
and renewer. "He heals the brokenhearted and binds up their wounds" (Ps
147:3). Renewal. Jesus, who has had a really, really busy Sabbath day in
Mark 1:21–34, begins the next day in solitude and prayer in the desert.

And Paul? Paul is Paul, he cannot help himself. "I don't want to brag,"
he starts, as he so often does, "but I have done a lot, 'become all things to
all people' you might say, and of course, done it all for the gospel." Really?
Does the saying "It ain't boasting if it's true" apply here? I do not think so,
because as far as I can tell from every other thing I know about Paul, he did
not change one thing for one single person in his entire ministry. I will be
surprised if Paul finds his way into this sermon.

On this occasion

Is Super Bowl Sunday an occasion? Liturgically, no, unless you live in
Pittsburgh and the Steelers are involved, or Green Bay and the Packers, etc.
While they will win the next year's big game, the local team, the Baltimore
Ravens, are not involved in the game this day. And as it turns out most of

the parishioners are Washington Redskins fans. We will more thoroughly discuss what constitutes an "occasion" in a later chapter. For now it is enough to say that a football game is not an occasion. Fútbol? Now that is different. Kidding. Sporting events, civic celebrations, secular holidays, and the like are mentioned in sermons, but they are rarely defining occasions. I am the preacher because it is "Theological Education Sunday" in the Episcopal Church, and while that will be mentioned in my opening "I am happy to be here" remarks, that is not an occasion either. The occasion on this Fifth Sunday after Epiphany is Sunday.

The provisional answer to the homiletical question

My hour is up. I have prayed and read and reflected, and I have learned over a lifetime of preaching that while I could continue to study with great pleasure almost indefinitely I do so only at my peril, and the ruination of my Saturday. So I make my first choice, one that is admittedly often too easy for me to make—Paul is out. And I make my second choice—I will likely focus more on Isaiah than on Jesus. Later in the book preachers will be advised to, at a minimum, focus 25 percent of their sermons on the Old Testament or epistle. This is going to be one of those times. And the sermon will be deeply affected by the contrast between frenetic activity and quiet prayer first felt when reading and praying over the texts.

My answer to the HQ is equal parts "gut feeling," what is already known about the readings, and what has been intuited about the listeners. It is possible that the preliminary answer to the HQ will be entirely mistaken, or that further study and preparation will suggest something partly or completely different, but after one hour of preparation what the Holy Spirit wants the people of God to hear is that one of God's greatest gifts to us is the gift of waiting, a particular kind of waiting, the kind that Jesus did and that Isaiah calls "waiting for the Lord."

Sermon for the Fifth Sunday after Epiphany, Year B

Like me many of you have lost enough weight to crush the winners of *The Biggest Loser* at the final weigh-in. But like me it is the same five pounds, over and over and over again. Like me last year you ran not one but two or even three marathons, but like me you spread it out over twelve months, not three hours. Like me your New Year's resolutions formed an impressive list of healthy eating, regular exercise, less television, better books, and daily prayer. Like me the first thing to go was the discipline of daily prayer.

We know we are out of whack. Out of shape, out of touch, out of time, and out to lunch. We want a trustworthy diagnosis and once-a-day prescriptions that will set things straight, put us, once and for all, on the right path to peace of mind, to permanent well-being; or at least to ten pounds instead of the same damn five.

I have good news for you, which, this being a sermon, you are right to expect. The good news is from the Gospel of Mark, but it is also from the book of Isaiah. The good news . . . wait for it . . . is . . . wait for it.

You live and work in the traffic corridor from hell. How is your stress level during the commute? For years I lived sixty-six miles from Sewanee for family reasons; the drive takes an hour. I have spent an hour on the Baltimore-Washington Parkway and gone half a mile, and that was to avoid the traffic on I-95. So you don't need me to tell you about the stress of commuting. Or the stress from underwater mortgages, job insecurity, health care costs and health care worries, what the market is doing to your retirement account, your kids' and grandkids' college funds—you get the picture. You probably use your DVR to avoid the commercials, but just once watch the commercials that are on during the national news—almost all of them relate to relieving the stress caused by watching the nightly news.

And then there is our diet. Not just that we eat on the run so we rarely enjoy anything, but when you stop and look at the ingredients on the label you cannot pronounce half of them. No wonder our bodies are so out of whack, we sleep so poorly, and take so many medications. Author Michael Pollan cuts to the chase with simple advice: Don't eat anything your great-great grandmother would not recognize as food.[1] I guess Cheetos are out. But who has time to eat right? Bill Hybels, pastor of one of the first mega-churches, Willow Creek Community outside Chicago, realized he was in trouble when he was pacing in front of the microwave waiting for a burrito and yelled, "Won't this thing ever cook!"

Waiting. You know a little about that too. Many of us have been waiting all our lives, waiting for the next big thing, for the phone to ring, for our ship to come in, for people to wake up and finally appreciate just how wonderful we really are. The list is as long as you want it to be. We wait to

---

1. "Six Rules for Eating Wisely," *Time*, June 4, 2006, http://michaelpollan.com/articles-archive/six-rules-for-eating-wisely/.

hear from the college of our choice, get the job of a lifetime, find our soul mate, buy our dream house, hold our firstborn.

Then we wait to get into graduate school, we change jobs an average twelve times per person, almost half of marriages end in divorce, we move almost as often as we change jobs, and then we spend the rest of our adult lives waiting for our kids—for school to get out, soccer practice to end, for them to get home from their date, pick a college, come home on vacation, move out on their own, find their own soul mate, and, if it is not too much to ask, a grandchild before we die. We know how to wait.

Waiting for the Lord? Not so much. Isaiah says the key is to wait for the Lord. But come on, what did he know? Life was easy back then: no clocks, no bosses, no traffic. You think so? Aren't we forgetting something? Like the destruction of Jerusalem and the conquering of his country, the years in captivity and exile, slavery in Babylon, and the conviction that at the bottom the people had it coming because they had broken their covenant with the Lord. So Isaiah waits. They have been waiting seventy years, what is a little longer? As long as you are waiting for the Lord. Waiting for the Lord. Hmmm. What does that look like, exactly?

Jesus. You knew I would get around to him. The author of the Gospel of Mark uses a quote from earlier in the same chapter of Isaiah we heard this morning to introduce the reader to Jesus, by way of John the Baptist. We separate what Scripture keeps together because, frankly, thirty-one verses is a lot of Isaiah to listen to at one sitting. But Isaiah has been building up to our verses, first by promising a Messiah, then by reminding us who is in charge, and finally by promising us renewal if we wait for the Lord. Mark is the one who realized Isaiah was talking about Jesus. And what does Jesus do? He waits for the Lord.

The first chapter of Mark, as I am sure your priests have taught you, is in an enormous hurry. Everything has to happen immediately. Can't get more contemporary than that. John the Baptist. Boom! Baptism. Boom! Temptation in the desert. Bam! First sermon, "Repent!" Call the disciples. Bang! Cast out a demon. Zap! Heal Peter's mother-in-law (didn't see that one coming). Heal and exorcise some more. Wham! Get up very early in the morning and go back to the desert and pray.

The time designation "very early in the morning" is vital to the Gospel of Mark. It is the time of quiet, and calm, and mystery. The time of possibility. The time of resurrection. For Jesus it was the time of prayer. It was the time to wait for the Lord, or really, to wait with the Lord since the Lord is everywhere and always. And it is the key to renewal. Have you waited with the Lord lately? Interested?

Spoiler alert—it is not a quick fix. But, and this is the miracle, the renewal starts as soon as you start waiting. When you wait with the Lord. Is the stress gone? No, and your mortgage doesn't get paid off, your kids don't get into Princeton, you don't get a promotion or a raise, and your health isn't restored overnight. You get something better. You get the capacity to appreciate everything you have, every minute of your life, every person around you, everything.

Now is the time for me to unlock the secret of how this waiting happens. I wish. The first resolution to go was the one about my prayer life. So let me borrow from a great teacher of prayer, who had his own struggles, the late Henri Nouwen. As you know, late in life Henri left the Ivy League to move to Toronto and serve as chaplain to a community of severely mentally and physically handicapped adults, L'Arche Daybreak. In one of his last books he tells of the person with the most profound prayer life he had ever encountered. Nouwen got around, so the candidates were many. But he did not write of Merton, or the Pope, Mother Teresa or the Dalai Lama. He told of a younger member of the L'Arche community named Jimmy, as I recall. For he would go out, sit in a double swing, and say, "Jesus, this is Jimmy." And Jimmy would wait with the Lord.

Jesus. It's me. It's you. Just us, Jesus.
Wait for it.
Wait.

Chapter One

Homiletical Exegesis

The truth is found somewhere between "The Bible is just the *Book of Common Prayer* taken out of context" and "We therefore have no Word of God but the Scripture."[1] But this truth also concedes that Anglican attitudes toward Scripture are just as complicated as in any other high liturgical communion. Which is to say these attitudes are complicated indeed. Yes, we do read more Scripture than many another church when we gather to pray and celebrate Holy Communion, but the multiplication of biblical passages only adds complexity, and one dare not brag about that to which one does not attend.

How does the preacher find a way through these complications? By asking, each time she or he is called on to preach, the homiletical question—*What does the Holy Spirit want the people of God to hear from these texts on this occasion?*

I argued in the first chapter that our best preaching begins by holding all four parts of the homiletical question together, and considers what this means liturgically, spiritually, pastorally, and socially. In doing so we have delayed unnaturally what we all do as preachers within moments of receiving an invitation to preach or our assignments in the coming preaching calendar: we look at the biblical texts. It is time to look at the biblical texts.

In the history of the last 500 years of preaching fashions ebbed and flowed, but one trend has been inexorable. Over time sermons have decreased in length, significantly reducing both the amount of attention paid to biblical texts and truncating the kinds of attention paid to biblical texts. There are always occasional exceptions, but when the typical sermon

---

1. Hooker, *Laws of Ecclesiastical Polity,* V.21, 2.

was an hour or more and is now fifteen minutes or less, there is less of everything, including Scripture. Nor is it only the length of sermons that has changed; so too has the ratio of biblical to non-biblical material in the sermons preached in liturgical traditions. It is impossible not to notice as one reads across the history of Anglican, Lutheran, Roman Catholic, and the preaching of other traditions. The greatest change has been in the last two generations, the shift from a focus on the text to a focus on the listener. One could blame this on Dr. Fred B. Craddock, but his sermons are full of Scripture while still being focused on the listener. So something else is at work here, and in the next chapter it will be argued that it is misguided and counterproductive. For now one notes that while Scripture is still important to liturgical preaching, it has a less prominent place in sermons. Which causes one to wonder which came first, the supposed increase in biblical illiteracy or the decrease in the focus on Scripture in our preaching?

Preaching is not biblical because it is preceded by three readings and a psalm, nor is it biblical because preachers begin their sermon preparation by studying those readings. It is biblical because the fruit of that study grounds and shapes the sermon as the preacher works out the answer to the homiletical question (HQ). Significantly, the preliminary answer to the HQ comes before detailed exegesis, and is based on a general knowledge of Scripture and on initial reactions to the readings in the multiple contexts of prayer, listeners, and occasion. Detailed exegesis allows the preacher to test, revise, confirm, and sometimes discard the preliminary answer to the HQ. This exegesis is distinctive, and while related to and informed by critical exegesis of scripture, it is attempting to answer a different set of questions for a different audience. Critical exegesis explores Scripture in light of textual and tradition criticism, historical and social-scientific study, and similar disciplines. Homiletical exegesis takes all this into account and asks one more question, the homiletical question.

Theory

The lectionary giveth, and the lectionary taketh away. Some weeks the preacher is overwhelmed with the ideas and possibilities of each text, other weeks the preacher will curse the creators of the New Revised Common Lectionary *and* the person who assigned these readings, even if the preacher was the one who made out the Rota. As long as the preacher does not complain about the readings from the pulpit, that is fine. In fact, most opportunities to preach come with more possibilities than the preacher knows what to do with. On Sundays one has a reading from the Old Testament and a psalm, the epistle and the Gospel, on average more than thirty verses of scripture. In the first hour of preparation these passages have been read and prayed over, and a few basic facts checked. A tentative answer to the HQ has been given. Now it is time to discover if that answer holds up to more detailed study of the texts. How much time? The specific amount depends on the total preparation time available, but the guideline is not more than 25 percent of that total.

A common mistake made by preachers at all levels of experience is to devote more time than is really available to exegesis. *Mea culpa.* There are a number of reasons for this—early on knowledge is limited, later one gives in to the love of exegesis and study, and sometimes the preacher is putting off the hard work of shaping and enlivening the sermon by the holy procrastination of exegesis. But the preacher is also burdened by an understandable desire to get it right. Preachers do not want to misinform or mislead listeners on a point of interpretation, and want to have the best possible answer to the HQ, the right focus for the sermon. All well and good. Preachers can still only devote 25 percent of the available sermon preparation time to exegesis. As many already know and pray to God will eventually have enough experience to confirm, the crafting of the sermon takes more time than is generally allotted to it. So if one has eight hours, then no more than two hours should be given to study.

Seven steps to a successful homiletical exegesis

The goal of homiletical exegesis is to test, confirm, refine, and if necessary redefine the preliminary answer to the HQ, and begin to sketch how that answer will take shape as a sermon. Over time each preacher develops a preferred method for accomplishing the task. Here is mine:

Step One—Pray, then reread the passages aloud.

Stop right there.

Stop.

If you are like most of us, you have already unconsciously decided to skip this step. You are busy, the texts are demanding, Sunday is looming. Who has time to pray? Good preachers. When discerning what the Holy

Spirit wants, prayer is a constant part of the process. Moreover, reading the passages out loud is a reminder that people are not going to read the sermon, they are going to listen to it, and so as much of the preparation process as possible should be oral (later you will be advised to try talking through various moments in your emerging sermon). What one is listening for is confirmation that what struck the ear as interesting/important/confusing the first time through remains that way. One also listens for relationships—where are the texts moving in the same direction, using similar images, echoing one another? The converse is also true—where is there a disconnect, a tension, or an outlier?

Step Two—Study the passages, i.e., "read, mark, learn, and inwardly digest them."[2] Choose one or two passages that are especially striking and begin making notes. Here one may have to make the first in a series of difficult choices, because it is not possible in the time available to do sufficient study of four biblical passages. So which passage or passages figured most prominently in the provisional answer to the HQ? The study should center there. For example, in the summer of Revised Common Lectionary Year A some may find that the childhood love of singing "We are climbing Jacob's ladder" leads to interest in the Old Testament readings from Genesis. Rather than trying to remember what verse follows "every round goes higher, higher," dig into a good commentary on Genesis. Study of Genesis will likely lead to the conclusion that Isaac, Rebekah, Jacob, and Esau may constitute the single most dysfunctional family in human history, unless it is Jacob and his twelve sons. While thought had been given to discussing how the angels got to earth in the first place since Jacob saw them "ascending and descending" (Gen 28:12) and not the other way around, close study reveals that there is something much more important to talk about. Alternatively, one might, on the Sunday closest to July 13 in Year A, be attracted to the Gospel from Matthew 13, the story usually referred to as the parable of "the Sower" although the sower disappears from the story after the first verse. If this is so you would choose the Old Testament reading from Track Two in the New Revised Common Lectionary, from Isaiah 55.

> For as the rain and the snow come down from heaven, and do not return there until they have watered the earth, making it bring forth and sprout, giving seed to the sower and bread to the eater, so shall my word be that goes out from my mouth; it shall not

2. *Book of Common Prayer*, 236.

return to me empty, but it shall accomplish that which I purpose, and succeed in the thing for which I sent it" (Isa 55:10–11).

The problem is that when one pairs Isaiah and the story of the sower one realizes there is a significant tension between the parable, where so much of seed fails to yield fruit, and the prophecy, in which this cannot happen. Now you are getting somewhere, your study raising real exegetical questions and making possible truly biblical preaching. It is time for a break.

Step Three—Take a deep breath, go for a walk, make some coffee, stand on your head, but *do* something, and then return to the texts and ask, "How will these words be heard by those in the congregation?" How do the preacher's questions, and issues, coincide with the questions and concerns of those who will listen to the sermon? What is going on in their lives, the church, the community, and the world that will impact their hearing? This is a critical component of homiletical exegesis, asking not only scholarly questions, but pastoral questions. And note again, this is not "instead of" but "alongside of." Preachers ask both kinds of questions. Is there enough convergence between the developing answer to the HQ and the concerns of the community, or is one in danger of preparing a sermon only an Old Testament professor will want to hear? As Harry Emerson Fosdick famously wrote almost a century ago, "Only the preacher proceeds still upon the idea that folk come to church desperately anxious to discover what happened to the Jebusites."[3] Just as preachers balance the spiritual, liturgical, social and biblical in the first hour of preparation, so here they balance the scholarly and the pastoral.

Step Four—Focus! Begin to look for patterns, overlaps, or disjunctions among the texts. Remember the old SAT questions that gave three or four words or word pairs and asked which one did not belong? Do that with the texts, and with both points of interest around and questions about the texts. When Sunday comes most preachers will have twelve to fifteen minutes, give or take. Some things are going to have to give. Ask, a la the SAT, "Which passage does not belong?" Ask, "What themes are most prominent?" Sharpen the answer to the HQ. One cannot, to return to the Jacob Cycle from Genesis, explore what kind of relationship Isaac and Rebekah may have had that led her to initiate the deceit in Genesis 27 *and* explore the idea that Jacob is depicted as a "trickster" well known in legends and folklore *and* detail the dynamics of "blessing" in ancient Semitic cultures. One finally has to choose.

3. Fosdick, "What Is the Matter with Preaching?," 135.

Step Five—Really, really focus! Ask, as if one had not asked the question before, "What does the Holy Spirit want the people of God to hear from these texts on this occasion?" If the answer is the same as at the end of the first hour of preparation, congratulations. If it is not, that's okay too, because either way one is well on the way. Another for instance may help.

One is preparing a sermon for Proper 17, Year C. There is a lot of sin. The golden calf in Exodus 32 or those "skilled in doing evil" in Jeremiah 4, with more sin in the accompanying psalm; the affirmation in 1 Timothy 1:15, "The saying is sure and worthy of full acceptance, that Christ Jesus came into the world to save sinners—of whom I am the foremost"; and the twin parables of the lost sheep and lost coin from Luke 15. The first hour yields an answer to the HQ that sounds a lot like 1 Timothy, what the Holy Spirit wants the people to hear is that Jesus will come and save them. But study of the parables suggests a different dynamic, as much as one loves the old picture in every church nursery in the known universe depicting Jesus carrying a lamb on his shoulders. The preachers notes that in both parables the one who says "Rejoice with me" is not the lost sheep and certainly not the lost coin, but the shepherd and the woman searching for sheep and coin. Apparently joy is in the finding. So the revised answer to the HQ keys not on the idea that there is plenty of sin in the world, and that includes you, dear listener, but what the Holy Spirit wants the people of God to hear from these texts on this occasion is more like, "Yes, the world is full of sin and loss and pain. We are called to reach out in love to seek and to save in Christ's name, celebrating together each week at the table to say, 'Rejoice with me!'"

Step Six—Reflect on the homiletical texture of the central texts. Are there elements within the texts themselves that hint at how they might most effectively be proclaimed? Huh? The idea here is that the biblical texts do not just give information and ideas, they give the preacher forms and dynamics, homiletical clues as to how the text may be most fully, faithfully, and effectively proclaimed. "Preaching" an agronomy lecture on Jesus' parable of the Sower is a mistake of content and form. If the dynamic of the twin parables of Lost Sheep and Coin ends with joyous invitation to join the party, so should your sermon. If Paul, in Romans 7, is wrestling with why his behavior does not match his convictions, pat answers are excluded. If one is praying with the psalmist this Sunday one may well want to include two or three extended pauses with an invitation to silent reflection and prayer, perhaps reflection aided by musical accompaniment during the sermon. The proper response to "Out of the depths I cry to you, O Lord. Lord, hear my voice! Let your ears be attentive to the voice of my supplications!" (Ps 130:1–2) is silence. There will be much more on this in the chapters to follow.

Step Seven—Begin to sketch the major "moves" emerging from the texts (see chapter three) in answer to the HQ and from thoughts about the homiletical texture of the texts. This is admittedly moving from exegesis to the crafting of the sermon, but when preparation is working at its best it should come so organically from the study of the texts as to be seamless. The preacher's one big idea, the answer to the HQ, must be developed in a way that allows the listeners to join in that answer, and not having had all week to think about the biblical texts, they need the big idea to be broken down into three or four smaller ideas, which we, after David Buttrick, we will refer to as "moves," not "points" in the next chapter. In the preacher's notes from the more detailed exegesis will be ideas, questions, images, etc. that may well have been underlined—dysfunctional family, joy is in the finding, what kind of foolish shepherd leaves ninety-nine sheep in the wilderness?!, the sower disappears after the first verse, late in life Paul is still wrestling, Esau's cry "Bless me also, father!" is so painful, etc. These are the beginning of the sermon development. Don't lose these notes, sketch them!

Like any method one will experiment and adapt these seven steps to best suit oneself and one's sermon development style. Here are seven caveats to these seven steps to suggest how this might begin to happen.

Caveat One—Use multiple translations, even though you will have a favorite, unless one happens to know biblical Greek and Hebrew. Even better, have on hand multiple study Bibles—Oxford Annotated, Harper Collins, and the Jewish Annotated New Testament—so that one can compare notes and not just translations.

Caveat Two—As already noted, resist the temptation to devote half or more of available sermon preparation time to exegesis. Crafting and developing the sermon should be given as much time as possible. And with the time available for study remember that it is usually better to go deep than go broad. That is, ninety minutes spent with one of the lessons is of more value to both this week's sermon and one's growth as a preacher than thirty minutes with each reading, because what is learned in that hour and a half about Paul or Ezekiel or the Fourth Gospel will extend to future sermons that focus on other passages from the same corpus.

Caveat Three—To again repeat myself, do not forget to ask the questions of those likely to listen to the sermon, and not just the questions of the preacher and his or her professors. This, like so much else in the process, is easier with time as the preacher comes to know intuitively what those questions are. If one does not yet have a good feel for what questions may be bouncing around the nave as the Scripture lessons are read, consider taking a Bible into the church and sitting in a different pew each week, knowing who will likely sit in that spot on Sunday morning, the faithful being as much creatures of habit and comfort as anyone. Then read intentionally with that person or that family in mind, doing your best to ask their questions while recalling all that you knows about them. A lost job, an impending marriage, recovery from a serious illness, conflict between siblings, etc. all impact how fully present a listener is to the readings and to the sermon, and the lenses through which Scripture and sermon will be heard. A student about to graduate from seminary, nervous about how her sermons would "connect" in her first charge, asked for a map of where everyone sat. Then, as she prepared her sermons, she moved through the nave, sitting where they sat and reading the lessons with one or two persons or families in mind, on occasion even using some of her preparation time to have coffee or otherwise visit with these parishioners. Contrived? Perhaps. But absolutely effective.

Caveat Four—Creativity cannot be forced, including creative exegesis, so do force yourself to take a break after the most concentrated study to allow what one has learned to sink in. Preachers quickly learn that sermon preparation often happens far from a keyboard or book, rarely on demand, and almost never on Saturday evening.

Caveat Five—While one does not want to be wrong, remember that there is no one right answer to the homiletical question. That is why on any given Sunday there will be thousands of different sermons, each faithful and wise, preached on the same lectionary readings. (There will also be thousands of terrible sermons, but that is not our concern). One must pick which answer to the HQ will be preached so that there is enough time to craft a sermon that is faithful and wise.

Caveat Six—The preacher really does have to focus, as much as one may feel (and perhaps been taught) it is important to address each passage that will be read at worship that day. One might "wave" at them on the way to the focus of the sermon, devoting a paragraph to each, but only if the readings are moving in the same direction as the homily, and you cannot linger lovingly over each one. Novelist Cormac McCarthy wrote of a priest whose path was so broad it failed to leave an impression. "And the priest? A man of broad principles. Of liberal sentiments. Even a generous man. Something of a philosopher. Yet one might say that his way through the world was so broad it scarcely made a path at all."[4] Do not be that preacher.

Caveat Seven—If one does the exegetical work well one will have vastly more ideas, possibilities, questions, etc. than one will be able to address in a single sermon. Like a film director who shoots more takes and scenes than can be fit in a two-hour movie, good preachers will leave a lot on the cutting-room floor, perhaps later posted as the "director's cut" on the parish website.

Practice

The few examples included in the theory section are hardly enough to give a feel for the process. This section explores two approaches to the same set of readings, and concludes with a sermon based on the second approach. I have chosen a Sunday in ordinary time, from Lectionary Year B. While Year B is the "year of Mark" there are times when the lectionary assigns the Gospel of John, most notoriously during five consecutive Sundays of readings from John 6, Propers 12–16. This section will look at Proper 15B, the twelfth Sunday after Pentecost.

In the Revised Common Lectionary in use in many denominations in the United States there are two "tracks" for the Old Testament reading, each reading paired with its own psalm or canticle. Track two is similar to the lectionary in the back of the *Book of Common Prayer*, OT lessons clearly chosen to complement the Gospel readings (and usually comparable to the Roman Catholic lectionary for that day). Track one moves through the OT more or less chronologically, attempting to keep OT narratives and cycles together over the course of three years. A later chapter will consider the basis on which to decide which OT track to follow. In this section it will be helpful to explore the possibilities of each track.

4. McCarthy, *The Crossing*, 152.

Track One

The epistle and Gospel are the same in both tracks: Ephesians 5:15–20 (don't get drunk but have a good time) and John 6:51–58 (the heart of the "bread of life" discourse). In track one the OT lesson is from 1 Kings 2 and 3 (Solomon's request that he be made wise, not rich or famous) and the accompanying psalm is Psalm 111 (a song of praise that concludes, "The fear of the Lord is the beginning of wisdom).

Step One—Read the lessons, and while doing so recall everything known about each passage, and what questions, one's own and those of one's listeners, have already occurred. Notice that the OT lesson is the result of some serious editing, skipping over thirty-five verses, and make a note to look into what is missing and why, other than length, it is omitted. The psalm is a joyous hymn to a powerful and benevolent God. The Ephesians reading is the end of a discussion of how to live as a faithful Christian in an unfaithful world, following the standard vice list, and preceding the *Haustafel* of instructions for the Christian family and home. The Gospel is just downright strange. We will come back to it later, but is it little wonder that in the next verse the disciples say, "This teaching is difficult; who can accept it?" (John 6:60).

Step Two—Study time!

First Kings 2:10–12 and 3:3–14. David dies, Solomon is king, and "his kingdom was firmly established." The omitted verses, 2:13–46, tells how this happens: Solomon kills or exiles all of his opponents, replacing general and priest with his own loyalists. First Kings 3:1–2 tells us that Solomon marries a daughter of Pharaoh, a precursor of the trouble that will undo him at the end of his reign (see 1 Kgs 11:1–13). First Kings 3:3 sets the scene for the dream in which Solomon asks for wisdom. He is offering sacrifices at Gibeon, a "high place" outside of Jerusalem. Here's the problem: Solomon is not going to seem any smarter after the dream than before. Before he was ruthless, vindictive, and self-indulgent; afterward he is self-indulgent (1 Kgs 4:22ff and 11:1–3) and ruthless (1 Kgs 5:13; 9:21). If he had not already killed his enemies he might have been vindictive too.

Psalm 111. Standard issue song of praise and thanksgiving, culminating in the commonplace about the "fear" of the Lord, the word (Heb. *yirat*) perhaps better translated as "awe" or "reverence."

Ephesians 5:15–20. Most scholars, including this one, agree that the Apostle Paul did not write these verses, but that does not mean he would not have agreed with them. Nor does the fact that he did not write it allow one to set it aside, as if non-Pauline means non-biblical. It is still a part of the canon. That said, there is really nothing remarkable about the passage, indeed of all of Ephesians 5–6, what might be called a "barely baptized" composite of stoic virtues and conventional Ancient Mediterranean wisdom.

John 6:51–58. The 5,000 were well fed at the beginning of John 6 and Jesus has walked across the "sea" of Galilee (it is really just not that big). All this happens on the first Sunday of the five-week sequence mentioned above. For the previous two weeks the readings from John 6 are one part "bread of life" discourse ("I am the bread of life") and one part controversy narrative ("Is not this Jesus? . . . How can he say, 'I have come down from heaven'?"). Pretty much all the territory has been covered, so in this week's reading one gets to, um, chew on it. Literally. This is the flesh and blood part of the discourse, Jesus offering imagery that even the disciples found hard to take. But there is an important, and I have come to think, decisive turn toward the end of the discourse, as Jesus moves from the graphic "eat my flesh" to the more important Johannine language of "abiding." See v. 56 —"Those who eat my flesh and drink my blood abide in me, and I in them."

Step Three—I am exhausted. A little confused, and I definitely need a break. You should take one too.

Okay. Ready?

Time to ask how one thinks the listeners may respond to these readings. The psalm should not prove much of a problem, although it might be fun to play around with, "Why does the psalmist want us to be afraid of God?" Nor is anyone going to be too shocked that the author of Ephesians (always the safest and most accurate way to make that reference) is against drunken debauchery and in favor of good hymn singing. The phrase is really quite lovely, "be filled with the Spirit, as you sing psalms and hymns and spiritual songs among yourselves, singing and making melody to the Lord in your hearts . . ." (Eph 5:19). Still, though, the closing line, while just as lovely, can be heard as both callous toward those who are suffering and just generally impossible: "giving thanks to God the Father at all times and for everything in the name of our Lord Jesus Christ." Giving thanks for everything? Who can do that? But this preacher has already decided that Solomon and Jesus are the most interesting characters this week, and in both instances anticipates a problem. With Solomon one may walk headlong into, "What is so wrong with marrying Egyptians?" and/or with, "Hey preacher, the Bible says Solomon was the smartest person in history. Are you smarter than the Bible?" Uh oh. And with the Gospel one will likely have to deal with John 6 fatigue, and with resistance to the graphic language of the verses.

All of these are valid concerns, and key off of something to be discussed below and in future chapters, the problem of hermeneutics. That is, preachers do not just deal with how to interpret (Gk. *hermeneia*) these verses. Preachers inevitably must consider how to approach and interpret Scripture more generally. In fact, preachers either talk about this, or talk around it, every time they preach. Does the preacher know enough about where the listeners to this sermon are coming from that she or he can address this or that issue, directly or indirectly? Has a foundation been laid to do so in prior teaching and preaching with *these* listeners? If not, suggesting that Solomon was not really all that great a guy, or that Jesus was antagonizing his antagonists, would be homiletical malpractice.

Step Four—Okay preacher, time to focus. The lectionary assumes a theme of wisdom, at least in the sense of choices that lead to living as God desires. Solomon chooses wisdom. The psalm praises God's wise choices for God's people. Ephesians says don't be a drunken fool, join the choir. And the Gospel of John says eat my flesh and drink my blood. I think I have found an outlier. Not to mention that after three weeks *everybody*, preacher and listeners, is tired of talking about John 6. I think I am probably going to focus on "choices."

Step Five—The working answer to the HQ is something like, "We make choices every day, and while some work out better than others, they all work best if we make them remembering that God has chosen us." While I can imagine drawing on the Johannine language of "abiding," I anticipate that this sermon will pay almost no attention to the Gospel for the day. This is not heresy. Always remember that Jesus managed to proclaim the good news of the kingdom of God (Mark 1:14–15) without ever mentioning anything from Matthew, Mark, Luke, or John. So did the Apostle Paul.

Step Six—The psalm will likely be the most important passage for this sermon. The "homiletical texture" of the epistle is a little bit of "this" and a whole lot of "not that." The gospel texture is full-blown controversy narrative, not helpful even if the preacher is squabbling with the council, board, or vestry. And the stylized nature of the dream sequence in 1 Kings is hard to replicate in a sermon. But the psalm is a joyous hymn of praise, pretty much exactly what Ephesians is calling for. Any chance there is a setting of

Psalm 111 in the hymnal or for the choir? No? Is there time to commission an anthem? Probably not.

Step Seven—So how is this going to unfold? What will be the key components of this homily that invites the listeners to make mindful that God has first chosen them? One could start with Solomon, who after all did make a good choice—wisdom. But enough has been said to suggest that this preacher could only do so while holding his nose, because I do not trust the stylized biblical depiction of Solomon in this passage—undermined as it is by the biblical depiction of Solomon in the thirty-three omitted verses mentioned above. It is never a good idea to preach something the preacher does not believe, even in just one portion (move) of your sermon. Start with Ephesians and mention Solomon in passing on the way to the psalm? Hard to do when one is not that crazy about the psalm. I'm in trouble. This happens, and sometimes it happens so late in the process there is nothing the preacher can do about it unless she or he happens to have mastered the art of preaching *ex tempore*. Fortunately, for the sake of this exercise, there is time to consider how the homiletical exegesis might unfold if the preacher chooses track two.

Track Two

The primary difference between the two tracks, of course, is substituting Proverbs for 1 Kings. The psalms are virtually interchangeable, and the epistle and Gospel remain the same. But there is a *huge* difference between the two Old Testament choices, setting aside the (critically absurd) idea that Solomon wrote Proverbs. Because Proverbs 9 carries no historical baggage, is a complete rhetorical unit, and is metaphorically in rhythm with the gospel reading in a way that 1 Kings 2–3 is not nor could ever be. The complementary nature of the relationship of the OT lesson and gospel in track two makes possible what this preacher's heart always wanted to do, and it is hard to fight against that.

Step One—Praying and reading, and in this case, reading Proverbs with great joy and the psalm with delight.

Step Two—More study! It is very hard to ignore the use of the feminine in the OT passage. Wisdom—*hohkmah* in Hebrew and *sophia* in Greek—is female, metaphorically and grammatically. And what does she do? She does what, in antiquity and around the world today, women so often do. She builds a house. She prepares a feast. She offers hospitality and invites her guests. Nor can one ignore that this delightful imagery follows on the "hymn to wisdom" of Proverbs 8. But more importantly for this sermon, she invites people to "eat of my bread and drink of my wine." Hmm. Sounds like the Jesus of John 6 may have been reading this passage as well. Psalm 34:9–14 is the conclusion of another wisdom hymn in praise of the "fear" of the Lord, and does not pull a homily this way or that.

Step Three—Although energized now, it is still important to take enough of a break to give thoughts and study a chance to either take hold or fall apart. By setting aside the reading about Solomon, and any conflicts with it, the sermon creation process has been simplified. Now, while still having to deal with possible John 6 fatigue, the preacher has something refreshing and perhaps empowering to pair it with—"wisdom" is a self-made woman who is throwing a party and inviting all of us to attend!

Step Four—The preparation thus far has facilitated focus without the clock—Sunday!—forcing the issue. Wisdom is throwing a party in her home no one wants to miss. Jesus provides the bread and wine, and the author of Ephesians brings the music. Wisdom has built her house. "Rabbi," the proto-disciples, asks in John 1, "where do you dwell?" That is, where do you "abide" (same word in the Greek NT). Not, as in track one, "What kind of choices are you making?" but "Where, and when, and how, are you truly present?"

Step Five—If the answer to the HQ were any clearer they would not pay us to preach. What the Holy Spirit wants the people of God to hear from these texts on this occasion is an echo of John 1, John 6, and Proverbs 9—"God has tried in every way imaginable to 'pitch his tent' right next to ours, to dwell with us, abide with us, no matter how things are going. Can we be present to the One who is always present for us?"

Step Six—The idea of a "homiletical texture" is often difficult to get a handle on, but the passage from Proverbs may help. While John 6 is wildly and multiply metaphorical—eat my flesh and drink my blood if you want to "abide" with me—Proverbs 9 is a straightforward, narrative metaphor: a short story. "Wisdom" is an independently wealthy woman who builds her house on a grand foundation, prepares a magnificent feast, and invites those who may not be quite so bright to partake so that wisdom might grow. If the preachers give a lecture on feminist hermeneutics or the varieties of wisdom literature in the Ancient Near East she has completely failed to pay attention to what the passage itself is crying out for: tell stories.

Step Seven—This sermon was prepared for a community not my own, but for the church of a Doctor of Ministry in Preaching student, a large and thriving Disciples of Christ parish in Nashville. Socioeconomically, educationally, etc., they are a prosperous, successful group of community leaders. And these, "Disciples," or as they sometimes like to call themselves, "Christians," have Holy Communion every Sunday. So while I felt like I needed to do some translation, for the most part it felt like home to this former "high Baptist." The "moves" that finally emerged kept the passage from Proverbs 9 in the background, but "wisdom" was always with me as the sermon went from "munching on Jesus" to what it means to be present to how we can be more present to ourselves and to others, and therefore to God, in our own lives.

A Sermon for Proper 15B

Eat up. Go ahead. Dig in. Eight times in the seven verses of the Gospel lesson we encounter one form or another of two verbs that mean "to eat," and three times Jesus tells us to drink. In biblical studies this passage is often referred to as "munching on Jesus." Gross? Irreverent? Sure. But also semantically accurate. This and similar exhortations led early critics of Christianity to accuse us of practicing cannibalism—I am not making this up. And it leads more contemporary students of early Christianity to compare us to a variety of ancient mystery cults, and to compare communion to other ancient ritual meals. Also true.

We tend to focus on the phrase, "Very truly, I tell you, unless you eat the flesh of the Son of Man and drink his blood, you have no life in you." But the Gospel of John may want us to focus on, "Those who eat my flesh and drink my blood abide in me, and I in them." Because the Fourth Gospel keys on the questions of where Jesus abides, and on what it means to abide in Jesus just as Jesus abides in his Father. How, to come at it in another way, is Jesus *present* to us? In particular, how is Jesus *present* to us in Holy Communion, and what does this mean for how we are ourselves to be present to Jesus and to others?

So here we are, maybe not all here, maybe half here, half at work, or at school, or across country with worry for a friend or a parent or a sister. Retired Candler School of Theology professor Tom Long reminds preachers to never forget that half the people listening to our sermons almost didn't come that day. Good advice.

But you are not here primarily for the sermon. You are here for the bread, just as the people, "the Jews," wanted Jesus to give them more bread following the feeding of the 5,000. A word here about "the Jews" in the Gospel of John. There is no getting around it, because that is what the word *Ioudaioi* means. It is tendentious, intentionally divisive, and a source of historic anti-Semitism. The odd thing is that everyone in the story except Pilate and the author is a Jew, including Jesus. If we recognize that fact it will help us read more faithfully.

We are all here for the bread. You realize that, and that is why you have communion every Sunday. The question for the author of our Gospel, as for Paul and other biblical authors, is *how* Jesus is present in the bread and cup? On this question we will disagree, which is why I am an Episcopalian and y'all are, and I know you love to say this, "Christians." There are more answers to this question in Christian tradition than we have time to name, let alone discuss, and a fruitful topic for a Christian education class or two. What matters is our shared belief that Jesus is *really present*. How that happens, physically and metaphysically, spiritually and symbolically, is where we disagree. But if we did not think that Jesus was in some real and meaningful way *present* in communion, why would we bother? Rick Lischer from Duke Divinity School tells of the time his Lutheran church was being renovated, and the architect asked whether they wanted an altar, or a table, for communion. They debated for months and said, "We want a table, but make it a big one."

I trust the Holy Spirit to handle the issue of how Jesus is present in communion. My job, and your job, is to focus on whether and how we ourselves are present at communion, and what that means for how we live out our faith.

Mindlessness is all around us, we just call it "multitasking." Years ago daughter Emily and I marveled at the guy we saw driving his Mercedes convertible to work and talking on his Bluetooth, *while he brushed his teeth*! Where did he spit? These days driving, talking, and brushing is for slackers. We consume banquets behind the wheel, text and talk, update our Facebook page, listen to Pandora, and check Pinterest for recipes. When we get to work we simultaneously check our email and voicemail, scan the markets, text our spouse and kids, and log on to see how favorite team fared last night and what Princess Kate wore. Sorry, that is so last week. Once home we kick back in our favorite chair, watch split screen television with the sound off so we can listen to another game or our favorite iPod playlist, thumb through *People* magazine while we scarf down some pizza and dessert. And that is how we *relax*.

You cannot do that here. You might be texting or playing Solitaire or Sudoku, but that is about it. Most of you, for just about the only time all week, are here. Present and accounted for. Take a deep breath. God knows we need more of that in our lives.

Consider food, since we have already been munching on Jesus. The venerable Vietnamese Buddhist teacher Thich Nhat Hanh tells of travelling with his host on a first visit to the United States and watching him eat a tangerine. Like the rest of his lunch, the man never looked at his food or smelled its glorious fragrance, ripped the peel off like he was starving, and tossed down a section as soon as it was separated, sometimes not even bothering to separate them. The whole tangerine was gone in moments, but there was not a moment of enjoyment or awareness. Sound familiar?

Instead, Hanh offers "eating a tangerine meditation." You look at the fruit, appreciate its lush beauty, inhale its wonderful citrus fragrance. You peel it carefully, mindfully, seeing the juice splash in the air, noticing the even more powerful scent. You separate the sections one at a time, admiring each bite before you place it on your tongue, and savor the fruit one bite at a time, waiting to separate the next section until you have swallowed that bite. What! Are you crazy? Do you know how long it would take to eat a tangerine that way? A few minutes. All to yourself. Enjoying and appreciating a part of God's creation, being thankful for all that had to happen before your enjoyment was possible. Really eating the fruit. Practicing being present. Take a deep breath.[5]

That, on a most important level, is what we are doing at communion. Eating and drinking mindfully, thankfully, aware of all that had to happen to make it possible. Abiding in Jesus, if only for the few minutes of the Lord's Supper. Doing this in remembrance of him. Take a deep breath.

Saint Teresa of Avila reminded her sisters that while the water for the garden comes from many sources—wells, aqueducts, rain, etc.—ultimately the water is for the flowers.[6] If there are no blooms, no fruit, why bother tending the garden of the soul? Holy Communion is, to use Jesus' metaphor earlier in Gospel of John, a spring that will gush forth into everlasting life (John 4:14). It is for you, but if it is only for you it is not all that it might be.

---

5. Hanh, *Peace is Every Step*, 21–22.

6. Teresa of Avila, *The Book of Her Life*, 114–84.

Your life, if it is only lived in the first person singular, is diminished; Jesus said that he came so that we might have abundant life (John 10:10).

To learn how to be more present to your own life is a great blessing. The more aware we are, even in moments of distress or sorrow, the more abundant our life is. But we are not called to live for self alone, are we? Imagine living in a way that practiced not looking away, ignoring, or pretending someone or something unpleasant is not there, but learning how to be more fully present to others. Whenever someone surveys former students to find out who their favorite teachers were they invariably mention two things, passion for the subject and being treated in a way that told the students they were taken seriously, paid attention to, cared for. Don't you want to be that kind of person in the lives of others, abiding with them?

Physician and author Sallie Tisdale has a wonderful article about her annual visits to a Ugandan village in *Harper's Magazine*. She writes of the beauty of the country and the people, the stark poverty, and the limits of what even a well-trained doctor can do in the midst of such need. She wonders if the people at the clinic would be better served if she just donated the cost of her airfare. She writes:

> What these people need is a different world, a new global economy, an honest government, a clean planet, peace. I can't even give everyone vitamins. But I can give them my attention. Suffering is part existential, made worse when no one seems to care. If nothing else—and often it seems that I do nothing else—I can try to see them.[7]

"If nothing else I can try to see them" is saying, "I can try to be present." You do not have to be a physician, or travel to Uganda, to do that.

Take a deep breath. There are people in your life, people in this beautiful church, who need someone to be present to them. Why should it not be you? There are people all around this town, in all the places you are physically present, and who need someone to be existentially present to them. Why should it not be you? Take a deep breath. Soon we will gather at the Lord's table. We must take what we learn there with us, abiding in Christ, and put it into practice in every corner of our lives. Take a deep breath. Be present.

---

7. Tisdale, "The One in Front of You," 52.

Chapter Two

Invention and Ideas

The first hour of sermon preparation is devoted to discerning the provisional answer to the homiletical question (HQ) for the sermon one has been called on to preach. The next 25 percent (or less, but not more) of preparation time is devoted to homiletical exegesis, which confirms, modifies, and sometimes completely refashions the preliminary answer and provides the first sketch, or more likely, a very sketchy outline of how the sermon might look. This chapter will consider a variety of ways to move from the now more considered answer to the HQ to the first version of the sermon itself. The chapter will be guided by and borrow from the work of what might be considered a homiletical odd couple, David Buttrick and Anne Lamott.

Theory

Most preachers report that their favorite part of sermon preparation is exegesis, and their least favorite is giving shape to the idea or claim at the heart of their answer to the HQ, the portion of sermon development that is the concern of this chapter. A bit of Aristotle may prove helpful here. In the first book of the *Rhetoric*, Aristotle defines rhetoric as "discovering the possible means of persuasion in reference to any subject whatever."[1] He goes on to say that such means of persuasion are found in three ways—*ethos*, the character of the speaker; *pathos*, the nature of the audience; and *logos*, not the "Word" of the Fourth Gospel but the *logic* of the argument in the speech itself. Later he will divide this logic into two parts, invention and

1. Aristotle, *The Art of Rhetoric*, 15.

arrangement. This chapter is about invention and the one to follow is about arrangement; both are about creativity.

But preachers are quick to say, "I don't have a creative bone in my body." In the way implied in that statement neither does this author. Most preachers cannot paint, compose a symphony, sculpt, dance, or write poetry and fiction anyone would ever want to read. But preachers do have an imagination, and are able to make connections between ideas, images, and listeners. Putting those two things together allows for a particular kind of homiletical creativity that is exactly what the task requires.

At this point in developing the sermon the preacher has a central idea in mind, the answer to the HQ, and may also have some supporting thoughts, images, stories, analogies, and biblical or historical examples that may help the answer to the HQ gain a hearing. But it is all still too vague. The ideas are still far from being a sermon.

A good way to start is with author Anne Lamott. In her wonderful book *Bird by Bird: Some Instructions on Writing and Life*, Lamott deftly compares and contrasts her two vocations as writer and mother. She did not have a how-to manual for either. There were plenty of books on writing, and about parenting, but they were not about writing her books or about raising her son, Sam. What she discovered is what most parents grudgingly admit: we don't know what we are doing but we keep trying our best, correcting our mistakes and, pray God, doing better the next day. Similarly, she found that writers need to plow ahead, because the perfect moment rarely comes, and the perfect phrase more rarely still. Therefore, she decrees that every writer deserves a "shitty first draft."[2] So do preachers. From Anne Lamott we preachers learn to take the filters off, stop censoring ourselves, and trust the particular intersection in our own vocations as preachers where Scripture, faith, listeners, and occasion meet to evoke the homiletical imagination out of which we preach.[3]

Pick a Proper, any Proper. When reading the lessons through for the first time preachers are struck by one thing, put off by another, confused by something else, and uplifted by still something more. And that can be from the same passage. What does one do with those impressions? Write them down, whether on legal pad or iPad. And following the example of Anne

2. "For me and for most of the other writers I know, writing is not rapturous. In fact, the only way I can get anything written at all is to write really, really shitty first drafts." Lamott, *Bird by Bird*, 22.

3. See especially the work of Dykstra, "Pastoral and Ecclesial Imagination."

Lamott, do not ponder whether the ideas or impressions are "worthy" of inclusion in a sermon, or even whether they make sense. Write them down. The evaluation of its faithfulness and usefulness comes after the homiletical exegesis and revised answer to the HQ. That is the time to reconsider the first and second impressions and determine which ones will contribute to the actual sermon, and how.

To explore how this is done consider Proper 21, Lectionary Year A, the Sunday closest to September 28. The readings are not especially challenging, nor particularly easy. They don't preach themselves, but they provide more than enough interesting material for fabulous sermons.

The texts do not line up in anything like an ideal fashion, nor is there any help from the liturgical calendar. If ever there was a Sunday in ordinary time, this is it: Exodus 17:1–7 and Psalm 78:1–4, 12–16 or Ezekiel 18:1–4, 25–32 and Psalm 25:1–8; Philippians 2:1–13; Matthew 21:23–32. The Gospel, from Matthew, finds Jesus teaching in the Temple during his last week and the "chief priests and elders" challenging his authority, an account also found in Mark and Luke, and the "parable" of the Two Sons, unique to Matthew. The epistle is the wondrous "hymn" in Philippians 2, and its introduction. There is no obvious relation between these readings, the lectionary is simply making its way through Matthew and Philippians. It happens. Nor are the OT and Psalm options going to help. Track one is from Exodus 17, the people of Israel in the desert demanding water; track two is Ezekiel 18, God's rejection of the proverb, "The parents have eaten sour grapes and the children's teeth are set on edge." Reading through the texts the preacher makes random notes, without self-censorship. For example:

1. Ezekiel—Why does anyone eat sour grapes in the first place?

2. Exodus—Didn't they just get miraculous water, manna, and quails in chapter 16?

3. Psalm 78—Why is a recapitulation of the Exodus event referred to as a "parable"/*mashal*?

4. Exodus—Wouldn't all parents be distraught to see their children without water? Then why is it condemned in this passage?

5. Ezekiel—What exactly is going on in the history of Israel at this point?

6. Psalm 25—What a lovely psalm; it is gentle and pious, but not over the top.

7. Philippians—A famous yet inconsequential debate: did Paul compose it or was it a "hymn" he knew and quoted? What difference does that make?

8. Philippians—Didn't Bill Hybels from Willow Creek use this to preach about "downward mobility"? (To a congregation of what, 20,000 each weekend at the peak?)

9. Philippians—There is more in the verses before the "hymn" than I ever noticed before

10. Matthew—Luke has a similar saying about "tax collectors and sinners" in the intro to the three parables of Luke 15—lost sheep, lost coin, lost son. And are not Matthew 21 and Luke 15 the only places we find the word "prostitute" in the gospels?

11. Matthew—Funny that John the Baptist suddenly reappears in the narrative.

12. Philippians—What about Paul's list of virtues before the "hymn"? Paul loves lists. Jesus tells stories, Paul makes lists. Could Paul's list be turned into a story?

And so it goes, almost free association. The idea is to allow the biblical texts to prompt the questions. As argued in chapter one, there are exceptions to this, but they are much less often than many preachers think they are. Let the interaction with the chosen or assigned readings for Sunday guide the initial reflection. To summarize the ideas thus far:

Ezekiel—Once again the verses left out of the reading, in this case Ezekiel 18:5–24, are both necessary to understand the assigned reading, and more interesting than what is assigned because it gives details and examples. If one is going to preach on Ezekiel, it will likely have to be on the entire chapter and not just the verses assigned for Proper 21A.

Exodus—This seems so "out of season" it is hard to know what to do with it. Passover is a spring festival and it presumably did not take them six months to get this far, especially without water. But the NRSV translation of the Hebrew word *rîb*, "quarrel" instead of "contend" or "argue," is suggestive.

Philippians—Whoever composed the "hymn" it is beautiful and important to the tradition, but it is not what seems so important on this reading. "Let the same mind be in you that was in Christ Jesus" is preceded and followed by actions, not thoughts. Paul never knew Jesus so how could he know what Jesus was thinking? It is a beautiful rhetorical turn but unless the preacher is planning on encouraging martyrdom, the list in the first couple of verses seems more homiletically fruitful.

Matthew—A controversy narrative (note the absence of the Pharisees —this is the point that they disappear in Mark and Luke, but they come back with a vengeance in Matthew) followed by a simple contrast "story" (this is where the Hebrew *mashal* from Psalm 78 is so wonderful—it means both parable and allegory, among other things, along with proverb, taunt song, riddle, etc.). The main thing is that the contrast identifies the reluctant son as the faithful son. Or does it?

No amount of study and prayer is going to bring these passages together into harmony. So the preacher has to discern, early on, where the Holy Spirit wants the focus to be on this occasion, for these people, and wave goodbye to the other texts. Because in this chapter the concern is more with a theory of invention than exegesis it is best to focus on two passages, the "parable" from Matthew and the introduction to the hymn in Philippians 2:1–2:

> If then there is any encouragement in Christ, any consolation from love, any sharing in the Spirit, any compassion and sympathy, make my joy complete: be of the same mind, having the same love, being in full accord and of one mind. Do nothing from selfish ambition or conceit, but in humility regard others as better than yourselves. Let each of you look not to your own interests, but to the interests of others.

The list of "do's" in these verses—encouragement, consolation, spiritual fellowship, compassion, mercy, humility, care for the other—can be understood as Paul's vocabulary of the gospel. Who would not want to live in a way that embodied these virtues? But so often one does not, which brings the preacher to the "parable"—who does the will of his father, the one who says "no" but then does what was asked or the one who says "no problem" and never gets off the sofa? One conclusion, if only in order to move the discussion along, is that what the Holy Spirit wants the people of God to hear from these texts on this occasion is that, "The God of Scripture is most often depicted as a God of not second, but of second thousand chances, a God whose faith in us far exceeds our faith in ourselves. What Paul asks of us, then, is not impossible. But it is extraordinary." Truth be told, most of this is really a recapitulation of the material in the first two chapters of the book. Now comes the fun part.

The preacher has gone from a jumble of ideas and impressions and questions through homiletical exegesis to a considered, if still subject to revision, answer to the homiletical question. How does the preacher then craft the sermon? In this case by calling on the work of the late David Buttrick.[4] "Structures" will come later; now is the time to understand one application of what Buttrick means by a "move."

Start with a simple contrast between "points" and "moves." Many were taught, whether in a composition class or a debate team, to organize both writing and argument by using an outline that had "points," usually three, with an introduction and conclusion. This looks marvelous on paper:

Thesis: God's faith in us far exceeds our faith in ourselves.

I. God is a God of second, third, and more chances.

   A. Example from the Bible—Exodus 17.

   B. Example from Christian history—Saint Somebody.

   C. Example from daily life—parenting.

II. Jesus shows us the way

   A. Example from the Bible—the "hymn" from Philippians.

   B. Another example from the Bible—Jesus giving Peter a second chance in John 21:15–19.

   C. Example from our daily lives—always ask, "What Would Jesus Do?"

III. We should use our second chances well.

   A. Example from the Bible—the parable of the Two Sons.

   B. Example from Christian history—just about everybody.

   C. Example from our daily lives—a troubled girl who grows up to be a CEO.

There is absolutely nothing wrong with this. This is, in fact, an outline for a classic "deductive" sermon that begins with a thesis—"Our topic this morning is 'God's unfailing belief in each and every one of us'"—and then proceeds in orderly fashion to "prove" the thesis. The case can be made that preachers do well to first master this form. And while the approach to preaching argued for in this book lends itself more readily to a Craddock-inspired

4. Buttrick, *Homiletic*.

turn to inductive preaching, there are times, particularly when what the Holy Spirit wants the people of God to hear is a doctrinal sermon on, say, the Holy Trinity or the incarnation or the nature of belief, that such an ordered, deductive approach is best.

But this is not very often, for these two reasons among many others: it is predictable and therefore boring, and it does not go anywhere, and is therefore boring. The sermon ends where it started, "And so we see, beloved in Christ, that God's belief in us knows no bounds. Let us therefore live each day in the light of God's love. Amen." The argument is not with the *truth* of the claim that God's love knows no bounds. The argument is that a three-point deductive sermon, while clear, is not the most persuasive. This of course is the argument the late Dr. Fred B Craddock first made in *As One without Authority* and supported in *Overhearing the Gospel* and *Preaching*.[5] He was and is right. An alternative is needed and, surprise! The alternative to a deductive sermon is an inductive sermon. More on that in the next chapter. Here the concern is with an alternative to "points" in a sermon. That alternative, from Buttrick, is to think and preach in "moves."

A move is not fixed and static, it is always going somewhere, and a sermon that goes somewhere, leading the listeners to a place theologically and homiletically different than where they started, has interest built into its structure. But an inherent dynamic is not the only thing crafting sermons in "moves" has going for it. Simply put, preaching in moves simplifies the entire sermon preparation process, first by breaking it down into manageable components and second by freeing the preacher from the dreaded "all things decently and in order," to which many are captive, i.e., first one writes the introduction, then point one, point two, and so on until (thanks be to God!) the conclusion. Most people, of course, do not think that way, nor can the Holy Spirit be relied on to inspire in that way. Not to mention how in heaven one expects to know what the introduction should be about until one has crafted the body and conclusion of the sermon, and so knows what it is that is being introduced.

Inductive preaching knows where it is going but does not tell the listeners the destination until they have arrived. In the example above it is far more effective to say, "God's faith in us far exceeds our faith in ourselves" and "What Paul asks of us is not impossible. But it is extraordinary" at the *end* of the sermon. Such claims are not theses to be proved, they are a

5. Craddock, *As One without Authority; Overhearing the Gospel; Preaching.*

conclusion to be arrived at. One can best arrive at the conclusion through a series of "moves."

A "move" may be understood as *a unit of thought or discourse, two and a half to four minutes in length, that makes a theological, biblical, or ethical claim and develops and illustrates the claim before reiterating the claim and transitioning to the next move.* This slightly revised version of Buttrick's definition has five moving parts.

1. A unit of thought or discourse. Each move is a complete rhetorical unit that makes sense by itself even as it contributes to the larger claim and flow of the sermon. If, for example, one decides that the claim "The God of Scripture is most often depicted as a God of not second but second thousand chances" is worth developing into a "move" one will do so in a way that is not dependent on any other part of the sermon in order to be understood and affirmed. The beauty of this for the preacher is that each move can be crafted independently, out of sequence, as time and opportunity allow.

2. Two and one-half to four minutes in length. The precision is an illusion, as Buttrick readily admitted in conversation, but it is helpful in a number of ways. The time range is suggestive of how people *listen*, as opposed to how people read. This forces the preacher to develop the move so that the claim has a chance to be understood, to sink in, but is not developed to the point of "I've got it, will you move on already!" It also means that the time available in the liturgy for the sermon dictates how many moves the preacher will prepare. A sermon of twelve minutes cannot make one claim ("Boring") or seven claims ("What? I didn't catch all that!") Each claim must be adequately developed and illustrated, but not beaten to death. Two and one-half to four minutes is about right. So, for instance, if it takes five minutes to tell a story, the preacher is in trouble.

3. Makes a biblical, theological, or ethical claim. The claim might also be referred to as liturgical, ecclesial, or historical. It depends on the sermon and what the Holy Spirit wants that day. But for the most part the larger claims are biblical, theological, and ethical within the context of liturgy and tradition. That part is simple, but what is a "claim"? It is an affirmation (God's love know no bounds), an interpretation of Scripture (if the father in the parable has *two* sons that tells us this is not a story about God), or an exhortation (what Paul asks us to do in

Philippians 2 is not impossible but it is extraordinary) that must then be developed to be understood and appreciated. The claim is what the move is *about* from the perspective of the one crafting the sermon, although the listener may say the claim was about the story or analogy the preacher uses to develop it. Just as one crafts the sermon with the answer to the HQ in mind, so one crafts a move with a clear idea of the claim it is making that moves the logic of the sermon forward.

4. Develops and illustrates the claim. A series of undeveloped and poorly illustrated claims leads to congregational head-scratching. (*Illustration* is not a bad word in this homiletic, although it is still out of favor.) Even when the preacher thinks, like Jefferson in the Declaration of Independence, that the truths of her claims are self-evident, they are not. Nor, for that matter, is the preacher seeking consent or agreement; the preachers seeks persuasion and response. At the end of the epistle reading, Paul famously writes, "Work out your own salvation with fear and trembling; for it is God who is at work in you, enabling you both to will and to work for his good pleasure" (Phil 2:12). People may nod their heads because they have heard the first part before, but they may also be thinking, "What the heck does that mean?" and more to the point "What does that look like? That sounds like something saints do, not someone like me." They need help in seeing how God is at work in their lives, and experiencing the hope that comes from recognizing that faith is not a self-help project but is a God-inspired and Holy Spirit-aided project. A lot more on this in the next chapter.

5. Reiteration and transition. The hope is that claim of the move, and not just the illustration, will be remembered, and that a way forward will be found from one move to the next without giving the listeners whiplash. This is also a topic for the next chapter, but for now recognize that both reiteration and transition come in many different forms. Rarely does the preacher repeat a claim verbatim, but sometimes. A silent pause is often the only transition needed, but not always. But one must always attend to restating the claim and transitioning clearly to the move as part of the "connections" that is a focus in chapter four, what Buttrick refers to as "structures."

An example is again helpful, returning to the "theological claim" that is a part of the answer to the HQ for Proper 21A.

"The God of Scripture is most often depicted as God not of second, but second thousand chances." At this juncture in crafting the sermon the claim is nothing more than an assertion. How might the claim be developed so that it is logical, persuasive, and something to which the listeners can not only relate, but want to relate? Moreover, what will be the likely points of resistance to this claim? God is not always depicted as giving second chances, let alone 2,000. Just ask Adam and Eve. However, the weight of biblical evidence is in favor of the claim. If the preacher does not think so then another claim is in order, and indeed all one really needs to do is thumb through the Bible to find example after example in support. There will also be experiential resistance to the claim. Not everyone was raised in a family or a church that practiced the "seventy times seven" of Matthew 18:22. Instead they have experienced home and church as places to be on constant alert, where mistakes are punished and forgiveness routinely withheld and replaced with, "I am so disappointed in you," or "God sees you even when I don't."

To develop this claim one needs both biblical support and anticipation of the likely shape of resistance to the claim. And the preacher also needs something else, something positive, something worthy of the listeners' hope and their faith. The preacher needs to *show* the listener what it looks like to accept some of those second chances, to live without looking over ones shoulder to see who noticed, to relax into God's acceptance. And the preacher should consider sharing what it looks like to extend to others the acceptance and forgiveness God has shown. It is not, after all, only about what is received. In fact, the epistle is quite the opposite, focusing instead on how one is called to live in light of what one has received.

This is the time in developing a move that the preacher must consider how this move may fit into the larger sermon, and accept that any one move is not the place to try to develop the entire argument of the sermon, but move the argument forward. If, for example, one is heading in the direction of a final move that claims, "What Paul calls for is not impossible, but it is extraordinary," the emphasis may likely be on providing examples of living in a way that practices forgiveness and acceptance. On the other hand, if the emphasis is more on the wonder of God's second thousandth chance, this move would focus on accepting the grace of the second chance, and not on extending second chances to others. To conclude this for instance, consider an early version of a move for a sermon focused on Philippians 2 and Matthew 21.

Not all of Jesus' parables are difficult to understand. Our little parable of the Two Sons is about as straightforward as they come. "Which of the two did the will of his father?" Duh, the one who actually did something. Clear enough, but what to make of his initial answer, "I will not"? Commentaries will tell you that this oral disobedience was unthinkable in an ancient Mediterranean culture. For that matter a strict reading of Deuteronomy 21:18–21 argues that a rebellious son should be stoned to death. Not that there is any evidence that it ever happened. Still, one assumes the father was not pleased. Oddly, though, this is not what the parable is about.

It is simply about what it means to "do" as opposed to "say." And somehow this understanding winds up contrasting tax collectors and prostitutes with the chief priests and elders who wanted to know where Jesus got off trashing the Temple. On the one hand we have the appointed and self-appointed leaders of the community, and on the other hand we have those collaborating with the occupying forces and practitioners of the world's "oldest profession." Stop right there. Skip the euphemism. Prostitute. Tax collector. Are these the "professions" first-century Palestinian children dreamed of entering? Easy to look down on those whose lives we cannot imagine ourselves ever sharing. Jesus shared his life with them.

Why would Jesus do such a thing? Recall what Simon the Pharisee said in Luke 7:39 about the woman who anointed the feet of Jesus with perfume and tears, and dried them with her hair —"If this man were a prophet, he would have known what kind of woman this is who is touching him—that she is a sinner." Of course Jesus did know, just as he knew what kind of person Simon was. And it did not matter.

Nor does it seem to matter in our little parable whether one did, or did not, do the will of the father. Jesus just wanted to make sure everyone understood the difference between doing something and talking about doing something. Ouch. It is so easy to get that confused, living as we do in world of good intentions. Our lives are full of "I meant to" and "if only I could" and "next time, call me next time." We give ourselves second chances all the time. Which is okay, I guess, because God sure as heaven does. Notice that for once in a parable in Matthew there is no "weeping and gnashing of teeth"; neither son is condemned. And notice that Jesus does not say the tax collectors and prostitutes will go to the kingdom of God instead of the chief priests and elders, but that they will be there to welcome them.

Where is this going, how does it relate, where does it fit into the larger sermon? Who knows? It is still early in the sermon preparation process. But the draft move stands as a rhetorical unit that interprets and expands the Gospel reading. This is important. Applying Anne Lamott's theory of the "SFD" the preacher can develop each move independently, as time and inspiration allow. Later, when it is time to pull the sermon together, the preacher may be surprised to find that there are more moves than can be used in this sermon, or that what was thought to be the last move is more effective as the first, or that this move needs to be edited or that move dropped altogether because it is pulling the sermon in the wrong direction. Craft first, edit later. Sometimes, okay, a lot of the time, one does not discover the true answer to the HQ until one has completed a first draft. Then one edits accordingly.

And this—it is not necessary to write out all of the moves. Many preachers find themselves with seven or eight interesting and important theological claims, and room for only three or four in the final version of the sermon. So sketch instead of write until one has a clearer sense of which moves are going to actually be in the sermon. Here's a sketch of the move above:

Parable of the Two Sons

1. "Who did the will of his father?" is an easy dynamic, a simple question—the focus is on doing, not saying.

2. Why I never! It's not nice to say "prostititute" in church.

3. Something is missing—where's the "weeping and gnashing of teeth" place?

4. Was Rob Bell right? Does "Love Win"?[6] Because it looks like everyone will be entering the kingdom (and why all of sudden "of God" in Matthew instead of his usual "kingdom of heaven"?).

These were the notes scribbled in preparation. Obviously not everything made it into the move, or was used in a different way than the sketch may have suggested. That happens. It also happens that entire moves disappear, only to find their way into another sermon, even one on entirely different texts. It is not as if the themes of "doing v. saying" and "second chances"

---

6. Bell, *Love Wins*.

are only to be found in these readings. Thank God for laptops and iPads. Preachers do not have to throw anything away.

Practice

The theory above recommends crafting the answer to the homiletical question one "move" at a time, a move defined as a two and a half to four-minute unit of thought or discourse that makes a theological, biblical, or ethical claim, and develops and illustrates the claim before restating it and transitioning to the next move. One example, from Lectionary Year A, Proper 21, has been considered; two more will follow, and then a sermon from Year B.

Proper 21C is a terrifying homiletical delight: Jeremiah 32:1–3a, 6–15 and Psalm 91:1–6, 14–16 or Amos 6:1a, 4–7 and Psalm 146; 1 Timothy 6:6–19; Luke 16:19–31. Jeremiah 32 is an enacted parable of return, the prophet ordered to buy a field to signal that there will one day again be buying and selling in Judah. Amos is a classic prophetic denunciation of the wealthy who think themselves immune from the catastrophe (exile to Assyria) about to befall Israel. First Timothy 6 offers a pseudonymous "Pauline" list of virtues, and the famous caution that the love of money is "the root of all kinds of evil." And in Luke the story of the rich man and Lazarus, whose fortunes are dramatically reversed after death.

Two things stand out in the first reading: the reader is not told of any particular transgression on the part of those whom Amos condemns, nor that the "rich man" in Luke 16 had arrived at his station by exploitation or dishonesty. Nor, of course, does the author of 1 Timothy say that money is evil, but that the *love* of money *leads* to all kinds of evil. As one sees in other Propers, the OT reading from track one is a bit of an outlier, the lectionary following Jeremiah rather than attempting to relate the OT reading to epistle and/or gospel. The preacher should not immediately toss Jeremiah aside because it is easier to relate Amos to Luke, and should certainly not do so every time this happens. As noted before and will be noted again, proclaiming the good news of the kingdom of God does not mean always focusing the sermon on the Gospel, or even on the NT. During the service of ordination to be deacon, priest, or bishop in the Anglican Communion the candidate vows, "I solemnly declare that I do believe the Holy Scriptures of the Old and New Testaments to be the Word of God, and to contain all things necessary to salvation."[7] Preaching should reflect this declaration

7. *Book of Common Prayer*, 513, 526, and 538.

more often than it does. One sermon on Jeremiah during the six Sundays in Year C (Propers 16–21) when the readings from track one are taken from Jeremiah is not too much to ask. And to complete this digression, when one does preach that one sermon on Jeremiah there is no need to limit oneself to the verses assigned for that day: talk about the whole of Jeremiah's life, prophecy, and his enduring importance for the faith.

The task here is not an exegetical exploration of all the possibilities found in the readings from Proper 21C, but to develop a move that could be a part of a sermon for that day. Having written elsewhere about the rich man and Lazarus,[8] but too often avoiding the Pastoral Epistles, it seems wise to focus here on the epistle. Before turning to 1 Timothy simply notice that while the anonymous rich man ignored the poor beggar at his door, the reader finds out in the second act of the story that the rich man knew the beggar's name. Hmm.

The problem with the pastoral epistles, beyond pseudonymity, is that the letters are such a captive of their age as to seem beyond reclamation, perhaps the best case in point being the verses in 1 Timothy 6 that precede the reading for Proper 21C, which not only affirm slave-owning within the church, but condemns "whoever teaches otherwise" (verse 3). Hermeneutics (principles of interpretation) will be discussed in a later chapter, but the problem must be acknowledged. Nor will the assigned reading be especially popular with many audiences. Consider these verses:

> 9 But those who want to be rich fall into temptation and are trapped by many senseless and harmful desires that plunge people into ruin and destruction. 10 For the love of money is a root of all kinds of evil, and in their eagerness to be rich some have wandered away from the faith and pierced themselves with many pains. . . . 17 As for those who in the present age are rich, command them not to be haughty, or to set their hopes on the uncertainty of riches, but rather on God who richly provides us with everything for our enjoyment. 18 They are to do good, to be rich in good works, generous, and ready to share, 19 thus storing up for themselves the treasure of a good foundation for the future, so that they may take hold of the life that really is life.

Is the author condemning riches? No. But the author is skeptical of the desire for riches, and abundantly aware of the temptations of both the desire for wealth and its possession. A person can be undone by wanting it and having

---

8. Brosend, *Conversations with Scripture*, 58–61.

it. Why? Here are notes on the way toward a move about 1 Timothy 6 in a stewardship sermon from the readings for Proper 21C. The parish is a typically prosperous, suburban Episcopal church, St. Swythns-in-the-Swamp:

1. 1 Timothy is a cesspool in which we occasionally find something of value, but if this preacher got to remake the biblical canon it would not make the cut. Paul can be bad enough sometimes, but "wannabe Paul"?

2. Is there anyone who does not "love" money? Perhaps, but there is no one who does not "need" money. Is the difference between "love" and "need" worth exploring?

3. The "eagerness to be rich" can result in being "pierced with many pains." Is this about all the stories of lottery winners going broke in a couple of years and saying, "I wish I had never won" and stories of people whose greed was their undoing ("acres of diamonds," etc.)?

4. Enough. Is this a place to talk about "enough"? Can "enough" be talked about too often—no one admits to having any limit on "needs," which is really a barely concealed term for "wants." It is never enough. Everyone seems to always "need" more than they have. If not now, when would be a better time to talk about "enough"?

5. How about a move that focuses not on those who succumb to the temptations the author describes but someone who is "rich in good works, generous, and ready to share"? It is, after all, where the passage is trying to take the reader. And this is a stewardship sermon.

Here is the proposed opening move of the sermon:

> If "the love of money is a root of all kinds of evil," what is its opposite? The hatred of money? I don't think so, nor do I think that is where our passages are guiding us.
>
> There is a scene in a movie I will never forget although for the life of me I cannot remember the name of the movie. Perhaps it is *Bonfire of the Vanities*. The scene shows a bunch of stock traders, self-designated "masters of the universe," discussing their "number," i.e., how much money they would need before they could retire. It is an old movie so the numbers would be much larger today, but as I recall they were eighty to one hundred million dollars. I imagine the film's (Tom Wolfe's?) intention was to disgust us, but I say "Good for them!"

Good for them? Isn't one hundred million dollars a lot of money-lovin'? It certainly is, but it is also something that many of us do not have—a limit. They are deciding in advance what their "enough" is so that they will know it when they get it. I wish I could say the same for myself. And if you are like me you know that you do not "have" enough, and that whatever your "enough" might be it is "more." Always. That's what many of us know; we know more, we don't know enough. And that is a problem, because then we can never, ever, be content. I realize the epistle's claim, "If we have food and clothing we will be content with these" may not quite work for all of us. What I am asking is whether you know, have ever thought or talked or prayed about, what you "need" in order to be content, so that you can enjoy it if you find it.

The second example is taken from Proper 21B, a crazy quilt of texts—the climax of the book of Esther or the story in Numbers of Moses' frustration with the Israelites' frustration with him, leading to the Lord sharing Moses' spirit with the seventy plus two and the memorable words at the end of the story, "Would that all the Lord's people were prophets, and that the Lord would put his spirit on them." The epistle is the end of the letter of James, but having written a commentary on the letter this preacher, oddly, does not refer to James very often—although if that is what the Holy Spirit wants, that is what must be done.[9] Reading and study, however, point to the reading from Mark, a notoriously "hard reading" preachers usually shy away from, what with the body parts flying and hell a-roasting. Those are great stories in Esther and Numbers, after all, so perhaps this is another opportunity to preach on the Old Testament.

Not this time. This time the Holy Spirit asked the preacher to deal with Mark, itself a pastiche of sayings found sprinkled in other places, and in some cases entirely reversed versions (for us/against us), in Matthew and Luke. The passage begins with an echo from Numbers, the disciple John alerting Jesus to the fact that some folks they don't know are doing good in Jesus' name, and asking if they should put an end to it. They should not. Then come the sayings about not hindering the "little ones" and the admonition to remove whatever causes one to sin—hand, eye, etc. The closing admonition echoes the salt saying from the Sermon on the Mount, and turns in an entirely different direction by concluding, "Be at peace with one another." Here are notes on the way to what becomes the penultimate move of the sermon:

9. Brosend, *The Letters of James and Jude.*

1. These sayings are always treated metaphorically. But what is behind the metaphor, and what happens if they are taken if not literally, with a more force?

2. How should one make sense of the juxtaposition of the salt saying and the admonition to "be at peace"? Is peace salty?

3. At least we all know who Jesus is talking about here, right? Someone, anyone, but me.

4. Where does this passage come in the Gospel? Chapters 9 and 10 are in between the Transfiguration and the "triumphal entry," almost no miracles, and one hard saying after another. When was the last time someone has dealt with how hard these saying really are?

5. What was that movie where the hiker had to cut off his arm to save his life? Or is that too gross? Or obvious?

Here is the "move," and a short conclusion, these reflections led to:

> Mark lacks the "you are the salt of the earth" saying found in the Sermon on the Mount, but he is after the same metaphor. Valuable, enduring, preserving, flavoring, all those good things are in us, and may come from us. As for peace, can we really justify capitulating to the culture? Does ugliness, disrespect, self-serving, self-seeking, I've got mine so the hell with the rest of you have anything to do with Jesus?
>
> One of the lessons we try to teach ourselves, our children, and just about everyone else is that "It's not about you." That can be a hard lesson to accept. After all, when most of us think about ourselves all the time, it is difficult to understand that everyone else is not fascinated and fixated on us too. They are not.
>
> And now I am going to confuse you. Because it is about you. It is not about them, and what they do and think and profess. Nor is it about what they do wrong, think incorrectly, and profess insufficiently. Jesus said, "You." You have the salt, be the salt. You be at peace, make peace. You.
>
> In the millstone-hanging, limb-lopping, eye-plucking part of the lesson Jesus warns us that what we do matters. There are some things some of us need to learn to stop doing. Specific, concrete steps we need to take to re-form our lives. They are not easy steps, but the failure to take them will kill us. Forever. So consider yourselves warned.

Crafting sermons is hard work. Anne Lamott teaches us to stop self-censoring and start drafting, because good sermons often follow on lousy drafts. David Buttrick teaches us that the most efficient, and creative way to approach the task is as a series of "moves," drafted in any order, as time and inspiration allow. When the preacher orders the moves, and crafts the conclusion and introduction, it might look something like this:

Sermon for Proper 21, Year B

Try as biblical scholars might, there is no getting around the fact that the gospel reading for today may best be called a metaphorical mess. You heard it just now, but you may not have been keeping score:

1. a huge millstone around the neck

2. amputating hand, foot, and eye

3. the fire of Gehenna, complete with a worm that never dies

4. being salted with fire, salt that loses its saltiness

5. and the greatest metaphorical stretch of all: be at peace with one another.

Really Jesus? Be at peace with one another? You don't have cable, do you? We don't do peace anymore in this country. We do confrontation—it's for a good cause, though, defending our rights, taking back our country, but mostly we scream. And that saying about who is not against me is for me? Lovely sentiment, but incredibly naïve. Matthew and Luke have it right: "whoever is not with me is against me" (Matt 12:30/Luke 11:23). That's the way we roll these days. Choose sides, crush the other guy, take no prisoners. A compendium like this, which textual critics and lovers of the King James Version note has a couple of verses—44 and 46—not present in the best ancient manuscripts and so not included in the NRSV, sometimes brings out the worst in preachers. Hard words from Jesus frustrate our best pastoral instincts. Every year when my middler homiletics class reads the first chapter of their first intro to preaching they are asked to choose between four understandings of the role of the preacher—herald, pastor, storyteller/poet, or witness.[10] And every year the vast majority says, "Pastor."

There is nothing wrong with pastoral preaching. It comforts, cajoles, soothes, and sometimes even chides. Okay, I lied. There is something

10. Long, *The Witness of Preaching*, 18–51.

wrong with pastoral preaching. It comforts, cajoles, soothes, and some-times even chides, which is all right if that is what the biblical texts are doing. Today they are not. They are confronting, condemning, challenging, and demanding.

There is another problem with a certain approach to the preaching task, a kind of vagueness that slides easily into irrelevance. In the name of considering a variety of perspectives, and in the hope of not giving offense for fear of alienating a listener, the preacher dances across the surface of the text, and so glides almost unnoticed by the congregation. That, frankly, is difficult to do with today's Gospel. When body parts are being lopped off with abandon, hell is simmering, and millstones are wrapped around the believers' necks, the odd quaint literary reference really won't help.

Jesus, you see, knew where hell was, and he knew how to get there. So did those listening to Jesus. Gehenna, the word in our text translated as hell, was the Jerusalem solid waste disposal site, perhaps even in Jesus' day. Toxic waste might be more accurate, given the identification of the site with child sacrifice in Jeremiah 7. It was a trash heap and a burning fiery furnace all in one, and in a really odd reference to the last chapter of Isaiah, this fire never goes out, and the worm in it never dies. Ashes to ashes and dust to dust, remember—the fire brings us to ashes, the worms reduce us to dust.

"It is better for you to enter into life maimed than with two hands to go to hell." Those are the choices? What exactly is Jesus talking about? Actu-ally we are not sure. One reading, more than a little over-determined and reflecting an odd mix of Freud and the recent sexual abuse scandals in our churches, considers the sins in view to be, well, things I probably should not talk about in a sermon. Maybe, and there is some support in the rabbis, but isn't that to take the metaphors a tad literally?

Of course it is. We love to do that. After all, if Jesus is only talking about four specific sins, something related to hindering children and one each for hand, foot, and eye, then if we steer clear of those four we are off the hook, and out of the flames. But do you really think Jesus knows human nature that poorly? Don't we have here a mix of the wildly metaphorical and distressingly concrete? Isn't there something here we are supposed to do, and some things we are not? Not an attitude to adopt, or a posture to take, but honest-to-goodness concrete actions. When Jesus talks about amputations, ponder long enough to realize that he might be talking about you, and me, and some things, concrete things, we need to change about how we live our lives. Or suffer the consequences. This isn't an occasion for a pastoral sermon; this is time for the prophetic. Prophets see what is going on around them, discern what is coming, and warn us. Jesus is warning us. So we sort through verses, noting which phrases are metaphors, lopping off offending appendages, for example; and which verses are not, like Jesus' instructions to John not to hinder those doing good in Jesus' name, no matter what church they belong to; and which verses are mixed, if not mixed up—the cup of water, for instance. Maybe it's a real cup, and there might be a reward involved, but it could all be symbolic.

The sorting gets confusing. We are here for worship, after all, not a lecture on the intricacies of Jesus' rhetoric in the Gospel of Mark. So let me make it plain—have salt in yourselves, and be at peace with one another. Mark lacks the "you are the salt of the earth" saying found in the Sermon on the Mount, but he is after the same metaphor. Valuable, enduring, preserving, flavoring, all those good things are in us, and may come from us. As for peace, can we really justify capitulating to the culture? Does ugliness, disrespect, self-serving, self-seeking, I've got mine so the hell with the rest of you have anything to do with Jesus?

One of the lessons we try to teach ourselves, our children, and just about everyone else is that "It's not about you." That can be a hard lesson to accept. After all, when most of us think about ourselves all the time, it is difficult to understand that everyone else is not fascinated and fixated on us too. They are not.

And now I am going to confuse you. Because it is about you. It is not about them. Every preacher has had the experience of someone coming up after the liturgy and saying, "I just wish so-and-so had been here today because they really needed to hear that sermon." Uh, "they" were here. No, this time it is not about them and what they do and think and profess. Nor is it about what they do wrong, think incorrectly, and profess insufficiently. Jesus said, "You." You have the salt, be the salt. You be at peace, make peace. You.

In the millstone-hanging, limb-lopping, eye-plucking part of the lesson Jesus warns us that what we do matters. There are some things some of us need to learn to stop doing. Specific, concrete steps we need to take to re-form our lives. They are not easy steps, but the failure to take them will kill us. Forever. So consider yourselves warned.

In the last sayings Jesus reminds us and commands us. He reminds us who we are, and tells us to live accordingly. He doesn't suggest living at peace with one another is an option to consider. Like a lot of other things he tells us to do that we generally ignore, he commands us to be a peace with one another.

Like a lot of other topics, we would rather devote ourselves to pointing out how others are failing to follow Jesus' commands.

1. Not this time.
2. You are the salt.
3. Be at peace.

Thich Nhat Hanh points out that peace is not a destination, it is the way we make the journey. Peace is every step.

Start now.

Chapter Three

Illustrative Material

Are good preachers born or made? Nature or nurture? Both, of course, but if preaching could not be taught it would not be. Yes, some students arrive in "Fundamentals of Preaching" with what is often called a "gift," but when one digs deeper one finds it is often one part a gift for gab, one part a background in academic debate or speech competitions, and one part the gift of having heard a good preacher for a season. No matter how gifted, the challenge of preaching Sunday after Sunday (after Sunday . . .) requires something more. It requires craft. Part of craft is asking and answering the homiletical question (HQ), part of it is homiletical exegesis, part of it is thinking in moves, and the part of it we cover in this chapter is the craft of connecting moves to listeners through story, analogy, example and illustration.

Theory

Ready with an answer to the HQ, an answer revised in response to homiletical exegesis, the preacher begins shaping the sermon by thinking and planning in moves. A homiletical move was defined as a two and a half to four-minute unit of thought, that makes a theological, biblical, or ethical claim, and develops and illustrates that claim before reiterating it and transitioning to the next move. The particular concern in this chapter is to consider in depth how one "develops and illustrates" the claim. Good preachers find effective ways to connect the sometimes abstract or unclear claim to the lives and concerns of the listeners, always remembering that the task of the sermon is to gain a hearing for what the Holy Spirit wants. Many things conspire to make it difficult to gain a hearing, and being clear about what those are helps preachers plan effectively to overcome the difficulties.

First, note that the rhetorical occasion of the sermon is increasingly unique, and give or take a prop, film clip, or projected image, entirely oral in a thoroughly multimedia age.[1] One person is talking, everyone else is listening, and in most settings where liturgical preaching happens, no one is interrupting with a question, a response, or an objection. Not even an "Amen" unless the preacher begs for one. This does not mean that such responses should not happen, just that they do not in most liturgical traditions. Because everywhere else in their lives people are accustomed to experiencing a combination of images, movement, words, and music all at once, sitting and listening to one person talk for twelve minutes or more is anomalous. One approach is to respond to the discrepancy between common experience and preaching by making preaching more like the common experience of the listeners. That will be discussed later. This chapter accepts that by and large there are only words and the actions of the liturgy to help make meaning.

Second, the listeners are anything but homogenous. Pray God they are racially and ethnically diverse, but they are certainly diverse by gender and sexual orientation, by family unit, by age and education, by vocation and household income, by interests and experiences, by ideology, and by the length and depth of their religious commitments. This means that while they all have gathered for worship in the same place, they come from a multitude of different places, and woe to the preacher who assumes otherwise. Just imagine a sermon at a baptism. How will the parents, godparents, and grandparents hear? The family and friends who are from a different tradition, or faith, or no faith to speak of? The long-time church members remembering when their children were baptized in a church on the other side of the country, and new parents visiting for the first time who are wondering if this is the place for their new baby to be baptized and their family to settle? One has to plan to develop the larger claims of the homily in ways that connect with the experience of a disparate group of people, who hear things differently even when they are hearing the same thing.

Third, even when one's familiarity with the listeners argues for a greater degree of homogeneity than is suggested above there will be important and significant differences in learning styles. Drawing on the work of Howard Gardner and his theory of "multiple intelligences," homiletician

---

1. Hipps, *Flickering Pixels*.

Thomas H. Troeger and his colleague H. Edward Everding, Jr. have shown that people listen to sermons differently because they learn differently, and effective preaching seeks to respond to these fundamental differences in how people hear.[2]

Finally, and this is only a difficulty to the extent to which it is ignored, each occasion brings a different set of expectations, always keyed and modulated by the liturgy while sometimes shadowed by the news of the week. When listeners enter a darkened nave and see the basins, pitchers and towels on Maundy Thursday they are cued to expect something quite different than the last evening when they are most likely to have come for worship, and are handed a taper along with the bulletin and enter a space ablaze with candles and filled with poinsettias and hearing a brass quintet join the organ for the pre-service music on Christmas Eve. So also when the font has been moved, or there are extra chairs in the choir stalls, or the chancel is stripped bare: expectations precede sermon in multiple ways.

The preacher has already considered how to respond to some of these difficulties and differences in developing the answer to the HQ, and especially in the homiletical exegesis, taking care to ask the questions the listeners may ask when they hear the readings, and not just asking his or her own questions and those of their teachers. At this point the preacher has some answers, both to the larger purposes of the sermon and also to the steps (moves) it is believed will allow for a faithful hearing of those purposes. Where will the preacher find the material to allow the moves and sermon to come alive, and to connect with disparate hearers, so that they experience the sermon as "profit with delight"?

"Rhetoric," it was pointed out in the last chapter, was said by Aristotle to be "discovering the possible means of persuasion in reference to any subject whatever." One clue to how to pursue this task comes in the ancient and modern rhetorical "handbooks." These handbooks gathered examples and provided exercises to guide the young student in convention and invention, practicing what was tried and true in order to know how to invent what was needed by the particular occasion.[3] The Apostle Paul was certainly such a one, based on his own testimony and the evidence of his letters. The collective wisdom of this tradition may be easily summarized: everything is

---

2. Troeger and Everding, *So That All Might Know*.

3. A contemporary example for preachers can be found in Proctor, *The Certain Sound of the Trumpet*.

available and anything is possible; the only limits are time, imagination, and experience.

"(Re)Sources"

The last chapter imagined moves taking shape, but the illustrative material intended to develop the move in ways interesting to the listeners was not much remarked upon, and seemed to come out of nowhere. It did not; it came from everywhere. Memoir writers are known to foster caution from family and friends, who ask, "Is this going to be in your next book?" The answer is yes, even if the experience or conversation is no longer recognizable to anyone but the author. The same is true of preachers. There are limits to this practice to be discussed below, but first we need to envision just how truly deep and wide are the possible sources. Students of rhetoric will recognize the debt to Aristotle, Quintilian, Cicero, Wheelwright, McLuhan, and Ong.

Scripture. The most obvious resource is the source itself, the texts for the day and the text from which they come. In logic this would be a tautology, using the source to prove something about the source, but that only applies to 2 Timothy 3:16–17 and arguments about the authority of Scripture. Here the task is to illumine, interest, and draw analogies that both clarify the "claim" at the heart of the move and provide listeners with various ways to connect with the claim and follow the logic of the sermon. Preachers do this regularly in at least the following ways:

1. Retelling the story. This is default mode for many preachers, which it should not be. But there are times when the biblical narrative is confusing, or for which background material is needed to provide an understandable context. There are also times when an imaginative retelling helps the listener "go" where the preacher wants them to, e.g. in the "Cotton-Patch Version" of the late Clarence Jordan. In her sermon at the consecration of Anne Copple-Hodges as Suffragan Bishop of the Episcopal Diocese of North Carolina Lauren Winner referred to the well where Jesus met the Samaritan woman in John 4 as a "pickup bar."[4] Gets your attention right away.

2. Connecting the text to its biblical context. Scripture is filled with antecedents, echoes, quotations, and allusions. Setting aside the centuries

---

4. Annual Papers of the Episcopal Preaching Foundation, 2013.

of complaints about growing biblical illiteracy, listeners do not often know what those connections are, or how one text is responding to another. Seeing such relationships is important for fostering a deeper appreciation of Scripture as a living, breathing reality, and also to the claim one might want to make about, say, Joel's reversal of Isaiah's and Micah's "swords into plowshares."

3. Character development. Lectionary preachers preach from snippets, especially from the Old Testament. When a towering character like Samuel or Sarah appears on the scene good preachers reach to all of their other appearances in Scripture to depict their faith and doubt and life.

4. Supporting a claim made from another text. Preachers are not limited to mentioning only the readings for the day, and if the interpretation of one of the readings needs support, elsewhere in Scripture is a good place to find it. So, for example, the story of the "Sower," the "Wheat and the Weeds" and the "Seed Growing Secretly" in Mark 4 and Matthew 13 do not occur on the same Sunday, but each interestingly informs the reading of the others.

5. Arguing against a text, or a problematic reading of the text. Ezra and Nehemiah say, "no foreign wives." Ruth says, "David's grandmother was a 'foreign wife'"! The book of Joshua tells of the total "conquest of Palestine" and the annihilation of all opponents. The first chapter of the book of Judges says, "except for all of the populated areas and cities." The best demonstration of the truth of the Gershwins' song, "It Ain't Necessarily So" is the bible itself, as the lyrics so magically illustrate.

This short list is hardly exhaustive, but rather suggestive of the various ways we use Scripture as foundation and illustration.

History and tradition. Often one of the purposes of a sermon is to suggest a course of action, a Christian practice or manner of life the listeners might adopt in their own lives. So it is not surprising that one of the favorite ways to depict or model such things is the "lives of the saints." Not for nothing was the go-to answer to every question in Sunday school either Jesus, Paul, or missionaries. Jesus and Paul are obvious exemplars, and so are women and men of faith outside the pages of scripture. Moreover, they are valued for their words as well as their exemplary lives. So someone like Teresa of Avila, Dorothy Day, or Bishop Henry Hobart provides a powerful example of how one might "show forth thy praise, not only with our lips, but in our lives . . . ."[5] History and tradition, it should also be remembered, is not just long ago and far away. History is being made today, and traditions are being kept, renewed, and passed on in the listeners' own communities of faith. In rhetoric historical examples were considered the most persuasive. Which may be why books and movies today will label, "based on a true story," whenever possible.

Culture. Books and movies barely scratch the surface. There is also music and theater, television and the Internet, fashion and art, haute cuisine and haute couture. Everyone lives and breathes, and worships, within culture. So everything the preacher reads, watches, hears, even what the preacher wears and eats, may provide a comparison, a point of insight, and a source of inspiration for the sermon. And then there are sports, hobbies, civic celebrations, all the things people have in common and many of the things they have only heard of—people know about the Super Bowl even if they do not watch it. Any and all such connections can be tapped to connect listeners to claim. Which means that just as the preacher must be a student of Scripture, history, and tradition, she or he must be culturally aware and engaged, i.e., should have a life.

Experience. Preachers do have a life, and it is far and away the greatest gift God has given us as preachers. Everything that has ever happened, every person known, every place visited, shapes the preacher's faith and is trying to find its way into the sermon. So pay attention. What the preachers knows, sure, and what she or he believes, obviously, but also what the preacher *feels*, what has been learned not just from books and lectures but from life and death. There are a million stories to tell, but as will be seen shortly, they should only rarely be told in the first person singular, finding other ways to make their way into the sermon. And this: it is not only the experience of the preacher that counts. Indeed, the preacher's experience is not as important, nor as plentiful a resource, as the experiences of the listeners. Because when all is said and done the experience needed to connect listeners to texts and to the answer to the HQ is not the *preacher's* experience but the *listeners'* experiences. Right? . . . Right?

Fabrication. Last, but hardly least as one grows as a preacher, is fabrication. Not lying, but making stuff up, like Jesus. To fabricate, in its original meaning, is to fashion something together out of existing material. Not *ex nihilo* but from what is at hand. We have extended the root meaning of

5. *Book of Common Prayer*, 101.

fabricate to a metaphorical meaning, to lie, and now the secondary meaning has pushed the primary meaning aside. Not in homiletics. Because the primary model for preaching is Jesus, and Jesus was second to none when it came to making stuff up. We call these the parables. And *parabolē* in rhetoric is one of the primary modes of invention. It works like this: the preacher knows what she is trying to develop in the given move, but try as she might she cannot see a persuasive example from Scripture, history, or tradition, or a helpful analogy from her lifetime of reading, watching, etc. So she stops trying to remember and starts trying to imagine. She imagines what it is like to be a widow, though she is not, or to be an immigrant, or as rich as Rockefeller. Some of what she imagines turns out to be memory, people she knew or saw or read about, but it only came to her when she stopped trying to remember. Soon enough she has a scene in mind, and because she is in charge, the scene unfolds the way she needs it to for her sermon. So as the listeners enter the world of the story she is fabricating (you can use "fashioning" if that helps) they find themselves being unknowingly sent in the direction of the claim of the move, and propelled forward in the sermon. It is what storytellers do. You don't know how? You never were good at telling stories? That is about to change. But first a caution or two.

"Limits"

Listeners generally love stories, analogies, anecdotes, and historical examples. The more the preacher uses the happier most listeners are. But there are limits to how many, how often, and what kind of stories should be used.

Length. If a move is two and a half to four minutes long one can rarely spend five minutes retelling the gospel narrative or three minutes sharing an example or anecdote, no matter how funny or moving it might prove to be. The illustrative material is *always* in service of the larger move and sermon, and the preacher must be careful to not let the story overwhelm the theological, biblical, or ethical claim it was meant to illustrate. Preachers must learn how to edit their own material to fit its role in the sermon. Everyone knows of sermons that are referred to as "My favorite is the one he preached about setting his pants on fire on his wedding day." It sounds like an interesting anecdote, but one wonders what the biblical text for that sermon was.

Appropriate. A good first rule: if one has to ask whether an analogy or anecdote is appropriate in the pulpit, the answer is "No." Not because of propriety or politics or prurience, but because there is almost always another example or story that will accomplish the same purpose without running the same risk. Some preachers like to be intentionally provocative on matters of sexuality, or think it is rhetorically effective to sometimes use profanity. Why? If one wants to be really provocative preach about love, acceptance, and justice for all God's children, regardless of all the things one might mean when one starts a phrase with "regardless." That can get you fired.

There is another sense in which illustrative material must be appropriate, and that is theological. Simply put, the images, analogies, and stories used must be able to carry the weight of the theological claim they are supporting. Cute things children say about puppies and kittens may be adorable, but just because "adorable" and "adoration" share the same root doesn't mean preachers should use children and puppies to explain the "Adoration of the Magi." The only real analogy to the love of God is the love of God; the rest must be carefully rendered as the pale comparisons they are. So when considering whether to use a particular story or metaphor, ask not only if it will offend, ask not only if it will clarify and illumine, but ask if it is theologically worthy of its place in the sermon.

Variety. Earlier in the chapter the vast diversity of our listeners was noted. The implication of this diversity for the use of illustrative material is obvious—illustrative material must be as diverse as it can possibly be. Preachers will always have favorite sources and resources, and their use must be measured and tempered (more on how to do that later). Remember this, if the preacher believes him or herself to be some thing or some team's or some artist's greatest fan, then by definition no one is as interested in it or them as the preacher is. One may find *fútbol* fascinating and the music of Keith Jarrett fabulous. Others like NASCAR and ZZ Top, tennis and Justin Timberlake, and still others find sports boring, are tone deaf, but have read the Library of America in its entirety. Preachers must vary their sources and resources, and do their best to keep up with cultures high and low, and because preachers will inevitably fail at this, if they do not have one in their own home, they should seriously consider renting a teenager. Not kidding—preachers will always be culturally and technologically two generations behind without the help of an advisor approximately fourteen to seventeen years old.

Personal. Most are familiar with the acronym TMI—"too much information." It is used to refer to inappropriate sharing of personal information and experience, and far too many preachers believe that it does not apply to the pulpit. They are wrong. It does, for reasons described in *The Preaching of Jesus*.[6] For the purpose of this chapter consider only that there are limits to how often a preacher should refer to his or her own experience, if only as a subcategory of "variety." But wait a minute, the careful reader notes, I just read that when fabricating stories the preacher draws on every aspect of her or his experience. True, but that does not mean it is necessary to share that experience in the first-person singular. And because one of the preacher's goals is to help the listeners relate the claims of the sermons to their own lives, it only makes sense to talk about them and about people whose lives look like theirs. A preacher might, for instance, want to share what she learned during a difficult illness earlier in her life. The preacher could begin by saying, "Some years ago I was so sick I thought I might die." Or you begin, "Many of you have had the terrifying experience of a life-threatening illness, whether yourself or a spouse, partner, parent, or child." The former has them thinking about the preacher. The latter has them thinking about their own lives.[7]

There are other limits, but these four are enough for now. If one strives to keep illustrative material from overwhelming the move, make sure it is appropriate, work to keep it varied and only occasionally refer directly to one's own experience, the preacher is well on his or her way. So it is time to practice.

Practice

The focus is on the fifteenth Sunday after Pentecost, the readings for Proper 14, Year C: Jeremiah 2:4–13; Psalm 81:1,10–16; Hebrews 13:1–8, 15–16; Luke 14:1, 7–14 (Revised Common Lectionary, track one). This is a Sunday where the preacher's attention is focused immediately—hospitality. In Jeremiah the prophet reminds the reader of God's hospitality to the people of Israel and Judah, from the Exodus to the eve of the exile to Babylon. In Hebrews the reader is specifically told to "offer hospitality to strangers"

---

6. Brosend, *The Preaching of Jesus*, 98–123.

7. Following the publication of *The Preaching of Jesus* the author was told that that this advice is gendered, generational (if not geriatric), and contrary to the desire of the listeners to "connect" with the life of the preacher. Because nothing is never and nothing is always in preaching, each preacher will have to decide when what has been learned in life is so personal it must be told in the first-person singular.

and teased with the thought that by doing so one may "entertain angels unaware" (RSV, but much better than the phrasing in the NRSV, "entertained angels without knowing it"). Psalm 112 rejoices in those who "fear the Lord" (v. 1) and who have "given freely to the poor" (v. 9).

Finally, in Luke 14, Jesus offers instruction in dinner party etiquette, and asks for behavior that he will later illustrate himself in the parable of the banquet in vv. 16–24, "When you give a luncheon or a dinner, do not invite your friends or your brothers or your relatives or rich neighbors, in case they may invite you in return, and you would be repaid. But when you give a banquet, invite the poor, the crippled, the lame, and the blind. And you will be blessed, because they cannot repay you" (vv. 12–14a).

Hospitality it is. But one has not really answered the homiletical question, instead is in danger of edging toward, "I guess I'll preach on 'hospitality' this week." The preacher must pray more and study more and ask what it is that the listeners will hear when the passages are read on Sunday morning. Where, one could ask, are the "cracked cisterns" in their lives? Where have they insisted on doing it their own way, and thereby resisted or even rejected the hospitality of God? What sorts of hospitality does this parish offer? Does it in any way show awareness of Jesus' teaching in its corporate and personal practice? What started out as a lovely set of readings on etiquette and hospitality, perhaps including Blanch DuBois's "I have always depended upon the kindness of strangers," is beginning to seem more edgy. What in heaven is Jesus really talking about in the teaching on where one sits at table? On the surface it seems like a ploy to avoid embarrassment and potentially gain honor if called to "move up higher," sound wisdom in an honor/shame culture. But is that all Jesus is after? Seems unlikely.

What does the Holy Spirit want the people of God to hear from these texts on this occasion? The liturgy is so helpful here. It would be much harder to preach on these passages if there was no Eucharist following the sermon. How should that be incorporated, not appended, to the homily? This, of course, is an exercise, and the interest is in illustrative material within moves, so for the sake of this chapter's theme an obvious answer to the homiletical question will be sufficient: "The Holy Spirit wants the people of God to hear about the joys of hospitality, receiving and giving, and to imagine together how one may practice it more fully." The sermon to follow will show one way of moving toward an answer. Before getting there we will consider three admittedly artificial moves, and envision five ways to use illustrative material to develop each move, from Scripture, history and tradition, culture, experience, and making something up.

Move One. We can make some really, really bad choices, but we do not have to.

The starting point for this move is positive, noting that it is a privilege to have choices every day, theologically (freedom of the will) and personally (the blessing of living in a country with great personal freedom, while acknowledging that for many the freedom to choose is constrained by poverty, oppression, incarceration, etc.) And yet if one believes Jeremiah people are as likely to make a bad choice as a good one.

Scripture. What one might do here depends on whether the longer homiletical trajectory in the weeks ahead included more Jeremiah, or if this is one of the few times he will be mentioned. If it is the latter, because the passage is so vivid and compelling, the preacher may want to stay within the text, highlighting the themes of Jeremiah while anticipating the themes of the sermon. For example, "As you recall, Jeremiah lived 600 years before Jesus was born, a terrible time for the people of Judah and its capitol, Jerusalem, because the powerful Babylonians were a constant threat, and would, before Jeremiah's death, destroy the city and carry the people into exile. In the face of such an enemy Jeremiah had the audacity to say to the king and the people of Judah, 'You know, this is your own fault. God has given us everything we could want from the moment our ancestors left Egypt, but we have insisted on doing what we wanted, not what God asked. You think you know what is best for you and your family, but it doesn't look like it from where I stand. Heck, you don't even have the good sense to drink God's living water just because you once dug your own cistern. Hello! That cistern is cracked. Really, before it is too late, make some better choices.'"

History and tradition. Choices have consequences, and usually when someone says that they, like the prophet Jeremiah, focus on the negative consequences of bad choices. Probably there is more than enough of that in the lives of the listeners, so the homiletical strategy may be to talk about good choices with great consequences. Rather than following the customary form of painting a bleak picture and then turning things around at the end the preacher could start with a positive example of a choice well made, perhaps from within the history of the church in which she is preaching.

"We do not talk about this very often, but none of us would be here if a small group of believers had not decided one hundred years ago to gather in each other's homes to pray and sing and read Scripture. This place, this community we love and loves us right back, was no accident. It was a choice, made by others, for us to enjoy."

Culture. The move suggested above is much easier to illustrate from culture than history, because it is fundamentally personal, and so can more easily be brought to life by recalling a movie such as *Babette's Feast* or the way a good but difficult decision worked itself out in a novel. In the book (and later movie) *The Hunger Games* the heroine chose to "volunteer" for the deadly "games" to save her sister's life, and set in motion the events that brought the tyranny of empire to an end. And there's always Robert Frost's poem, "The Road Not Taken."

Experience. Many people hate choices because they are afraid they will make the wrong choice. So they make the choice of not choosing and hope for the best. Jeremiah says that this strategy is not going to work anymore. It is easy to tell of the dire consequences of choices not made, so the listeners may have heard that sermon. What about a difference approach, asking, "Did you ever make supper for an angel? What do angels eat, anyway? The Bible calls manna the 'bread of angels' but the people of Israel sure got tired of it in a hurry." Invite them to recall a good choice made by someone they know. How did that work out? Some years ago a woman in the community approached a church and its pastor to see if help might be found for a shelter for homeless women and their children. After some hesitation the governing body agreed, and the church members rushed in "where angels fear to tread," giving, collecting, building, welcoming. Angels were definitely entertained. Tell that story.

Fabrication. By now the reader may be beginning to see why the author is so fond of fabrication. It does not require double-checking facts, correct spelling, or precise details. One does not have to worry about confidentiality or historicity. The preacher, for example, knows that she wants to show what it feels like to receive the gift of hospitality, and perhaps what it feels like when there is no hospitality to be found. In all likelihood she has experienced both. So she draws on her experience, in particular what she felt and the truth she learned, and then recast it as someone else's story. This is what will be found in the opening paragraphs of the sermon at chapter's end.

Move Two. We need to work on our social skills.

The claim of this move is ethical. People know at least nine times out of ten what they are "supposed" to do, but they do not do it. Why? Because they are miserable sinners? Not in this move. In this move they are unskilled, ungracious, and a little bit prejudiced, but they *mean* well. Here are some ways to illustrate this claim:

Scripture. The possibilities are great, from Joshua 24's "choose this day whom you will serve" to Paul's "I do not know what I do" in Romans 7 to Jesus' parable of the Two Sons in Matthew 21. There is the "two ways" wisdom tradition found at the beginning of the *Didache* and in the little parable of the two houses at the end of the Sermon on the Mount, light and darkness in the Fourth Gospel, sins of the flesh and fruits of the Spirit in Galatians, and of course law and gospel.

History and tradition. Hmm. Any difficult choices in history, be it church or otherwise? Any anecdotes one can recall about persons, communities or nations confronting difficult choices, knowing what is the right thing to do and choosing the wrong or right thing, depending on what direction you want to go in the sermon. For instance, human slavery; this author teaches at *The* University of the South, so slavery remains a fraught issue, the same with Jim Crow, old and new. One wants to believe that when all was said and done folks around the country and around the world knew what was the *right* thing to do, but it was difficult, involved some self-sacrifice and a significant setting aside of self-interest. Perhaps a story about the Underground Railroad and "welcoming the stranger" in dangerous circumstances would be in order.

Culture. Think self-help literature, whatever the topic: weight loss? Eat less junk, more veggies, and exercise; everyone knows what to do. Happy marriage? Trust, communication, shared responsibilities around the house and in raising the children, date nights; everyone knows what to do. Parenting? Boundaries and discipline, time and affection, consistency; everyone knows what to do. One could go on but the point is obvious. Nine times out of ten everyone knows what to do but does not do it. So billions of dollars are spent on books, podcasts, etc. to motivate folks to do what they know they should do. People act as if the choice is between using time they do not have to prepare healthy meals or going to McDonalds, or between carrot sticks and Twinkies, when it is really between daily or occasional McDonalds, and one Twinkie or two. It is really not that hard.

Experience. This is *not* the time to overshare. Preachers undoubtedly have tales to tell of indecision, bad choices, regrets. So does everyone else, so why concentrate on the preacher's own? The claim of this move is that one knows what to do but regularly does not do it. Because nothing is never and nothing is always in preaching, now might be the time to bring out the cute things children say, a lá *The Emperor's New Clothes*, when a child's honesty shamed the adults into recognizing their hypocrisy and forced them to do the right thing.

Fabrication. The experience of indecision, of pretending to not know what to do, is all around. So take something well known, mix it with something personally experienced, and point it in the direction the preacher wants the sermon to go, toward hospitality. For instance, "One of the things that keeps us from opening our hearts, and our doors, to the stranger is that we are not sure what will happen, and whenever we are not sure what will happen we usually only imagine the worst, and rarely the best. That was certainly true of the Smiths when their daughter came home from school with a flyer about hosting a foreign exchange student. 'How do we know they are who they say they are?' and 'What if they don't like it here?' and 'Where will your grandparents stay at Thanksgiving if the foreigner gets the guest room?' Yes, it is as pathetic as it sounds. Daughter pointed out that they could not very well expect someone to welcome her in a year or two when she went abroad if they were not willing to do the same, and so shamed her parents into attending the information meeting. You know how this ends, right? They reluctantly agreed, welcomed the sixteen-year-old girl from Argentina into their home, then into their lives, and finally into their hearts, and gained a second daughter, her family, and a country in the bargain." Or maybe fashion a story about foster care. That works too.

Move Three. The joys of receiving and giving.

This, perhaps but not necessarily final move, is also ethical, and practical, with the goal of helping the listener *feel* the joy of hospitality the preacher believes may be the real gift of God's hospitality, not doing it all for us, so that we may enjoy offering holy hospitality to others.

Scripture. Who did the author of the Letter to the Hebrews have in mind when talking about "angels unaware"? Abraham and Sarah in Genesis 18? Lot in the chapter to follow? How about Cleopas and his companion (wife?) on the Emmaus Road? Maybe not angels, but how did other acts of hospitality in scripture work out? Zacchaeus seemed pretty happy and he didn't even do the inviting, Jesus invited himself. And there is the "Rejoice with me!" of the man who found his lost sheep and the woman who found her coin in Luke 15, inviting neighbors to share in the joy of discovery. The converse is also true, for those who do not offer hospitality often suffer the consequences (the rich man who ignored Lazarus in Luke 16, for example). But the preacher probably wants to stay positive at this point, even if the sermon did not start off that way.

History and tradition. Any famous acts of hospitality beyond the "first" Thanksgiving come to mind? Then maybe turn to the traditions of the Lord's table, and the struggles over who was or was not welcome that inevitably turn toward inclusion, and always turned out better for it.

Culture. This is exactly what Jesus is after in the "invite the poor" saying. Contemporary culture does a fabulous job of offering superficial hospitality. It is practically sanctioned, especially during the holidays, as every athlete and singer on the planet goes to the hospital to visit the sick little kids at Christmas. What happens when the children are discharged? Anybody helping out with their bills or co-pay? Didn't think so. Here one can imagine puncturing the pretensions of "caring" fostered in our culture to clear the way for something deeper.

Experience. Speaking of something deeper, consider this: in the barrio (*colonias*) of Juarez is a poor woman who lives proudly in a cinder block house with electricity coming from an extension cord connected to her neighbor's house, who is connected by a wire dangling from a pole across the "street," actually just the sandy stretch in between houses. She has a fourth grade education, and her husband works in the *maquiladores* assembling whatever comes down the line. Down the street, with some help from a group of Columbian Fathers they have built a house out of hay bales and adobe (cheap *and* insulated) in which they have a library, an after school tutoring program, and a three times a week program for special needs children—autism, spina-bifida, Down Syndrome, etc. At the edge of the universe, poverty and drug-cartel violence central, this woman and her small community offer hospitality to special needs kids, their siblings, and their families. *Magnifico!*

Fabrication. One could not make up a story of hospitality better than the one seen in Juarez. So here is one not as good. A priest is driving home after a busy Sunday morning of worship and formation, visions of an afternoon of doing nothing dancing in her head. As she approaches the busy interstate intersection she sees a homeless guy with a cardboard sign beside the road, and she freezes. To help or not to help? And what exactly would be helped anyway? What this person needs is a job, maybe rehab, obviously health care, probably mental health care. The horn honking behind her brings an end to these deliberations and she lurches forward a few car lengths past the homeless guy. Looking for him in the rearview mirror she notices someone in the car behind and in the curb lane getting out of her car. It is her seventy-eight-year-old parishioner, Marsha. The light changes and cars honk and Marsha calmly touches the homeless man gently on the shoulder, hands him five dollars, and seems to be bowing her head in prayer. Then she gets in her car, waving at the people honking at her, smiling. And do you know how good God is? A few blocks later there was another homeless person, with her own sign, and the priest pulled over, and went to her, and smiled, introduced herself, and asked how she could help her today.

What was that all about? It was an attempt to suggest that for any given move the theological, biblical, or ethical claim can be developed through any number of sources and resources, but principally Scripture, history and tradition, culture, experience, and making stuff up. Perhaps the most obvious evidence of the exercise is that not every resource works equally well, and just as the answer to the HQ includes attention to the homiletical texture of the texts for the day, the nature of the claim at the heart of the move suggests where the preacher should first look for supportive and illustrative material. How this is *arranged*, refashioned, introduced, and concluded is the topic in the next chapter. But first the sermon that was the end product of the exercise.

Sermon for the fifteenth Sunday after Pentecost, Proper 17, Year C

The woman was lost in a country not her own, with scant skill in the language, and all she wanted to do was go to church. How hard could that be? Armed with a map she barely understood, an address, and the name of the pastor of the *Evangelische Freikirche*, she missed her bus stop, and things went downhill from there. Finally, she found the right intersection, turned the corner, and as she walked up the steps to the church she was met by a host of people walking out the doors. Great, she thought, I missed the service. Using what little German she knew she pointed to the piece of paper with the pastor's name. *"Sommerferien"* she was told—on summer vacation. Crestfallen, she stuffed papers and map into her purse and began to retrace her steps when someone tapped her on the shoulder and said, "Hello! Are you from America?" In English far superior to her German, the woman was invited to share her story, then invited home to share lunch with a large and friendly family, followed by a bicycle tour of the city, drinks and snacks in a café, and a late afternoon escort to the train station. What began so badly became one of the best days of her life, and the highlight of her trip.

On another corner in another part of the world a man in a wheelchair was not doing so well. Americans with Disabilities Act notwithstanding, there were no cuts in the curb, and no ramp to the building. At least he could appreciate the bitter, perfect irony—he could not get across the street, or enter the building to see the lawyer handling his suit for workplace discrimination and accommodation.

School's started. It had been almost two weeks, and the shy new student remained overwhelmed by his situation. He roomed alone, sat by himself in the cafeteria, was afraid to speak in class, and the only conversation he recalled having in days was at the library to ask for a reserve book. He had been told this was such a friendly place, which was part of the reason he came to this school instead of one offering better financial aid. But so far the friendliness had passed him by. Whatever happened to Southern hospitality?

The children of Jacob came as guests, accepting Egyptian hospitality. That didn't last long, though, because a "Pharaoh who knew not Joseph" had big plans and needed lots of cheap labor. Centuries pass, cries were heard, Moses was sent, and Pharaoh finally let God's people go, a decision God soon regretted and, well, you know that story. So did Jeremiah. God, said the prophet, was deliverer, welcomer, and host, "Open your mouth wide, and I will fill it," says the Lord. But the people of Israel and Judah thought otherwise, made other plans, preferred other nourishment. More than anything, the narratives suggest that the story of God's deliverance was repeatedly translated into a self-salvation, up by the bootstraps, I-did-it-my-way sort of tale. In Jeremiah's damning image the people were so determined to do it for themselves they preferred fetid water from cracked cisterns to the living water of the creator God.

Jesus noticed something similar sitting at the Pharisee's table, folk preferring social reciprocity to holy hospitality. The New Testament scholar notes that Jesus did not repudiate the Ancient Mediterranean patronage system and honor/shame culture that provides the socioeconomic background to the story, but as a teacher of alternative wisdom Jesus gave both patronage and honor a decisive twist.

The pages of Scripture are filled with the hospitality of God. As Eucharistic Prayer B begins, "We give thanks to you, O God, for the goodness and love which you have made known to us in creation; in the calling of Israel to be your people, in your Word spoken through the prophets; and above all in your Word made flesh, Jesus, your Son."[8] In fact, about the only thing more prevalent in Scripture and the history of the church than the hospitality of God is our refusal to accept it. As strange as it seems, whenever we stop and think about it we have a really hard time saying "Yes" to God. God says, "Would you like a nice, cool sip of living water?" and we say, "No, I've got a well I dug my very own self. It's cracked, polluted, and the water in it just may kill me, but it's mine."

God says, "Do me a favor, take care of each other. I'm especially worried about the widows and orphans, the homeless and helpless, the ones who tend to get overlooked and ignored by society, so I'm counting on you people of faith to take care of them." And we say, "I don't see anyone like that around here. And besides, it's a *family* reunion, a *business* dinner, a *church* potluck. People like that don't really belong. I'm sure they wouldn't be comfortable." God says, "Love me and love your neighbor." We say, "Who is my neighbor?" How in heaven did that happen? Why does it still happen? The Letter of Hebrews asks us to practice *philoxenia*—love of the stranger (13:2). *Xenophobia* is not exactly a substitute. Nor are any of the other phobias a preacher might mention right about now.

How does this happen? How can we good Christian people so persistently set aside the words of the prophets Jeremiah and Jesus? Because we don't believe them. I realize that is quite a claim but it must be true. We know the words, we acknowledge them, we even affirm the words in the Creeds, but if we are not living them, in what meaningful way may we be said to "have faith in" the words of Scripture?

Here's the catch, and stay with me because this is not going to be pleasant. There is one central way in which we do not have faith in the divine hospitality, which leads to a second thing that really gets us spiraling down: we believe all kinds of things in the abstract. We may even believe it about others. Where we trip and stumble is all over *ourselves*—we are our own stumbling block, because we cannot believe that God's hospitality, that

8. *Book of Common Prayer*, 368.

Christ's welcome, is finally very personal, and that the person is *me*. When it comes to *Gastfreundschaft*, *philoxenia*, and hospitality, we usually fail to reach *out* to the stranger because we cannot reach *in* to our own hearts. If we don't welcome ourselves just how good are we going to ever be at welcoming others? If we don't accept Christ's welcome of us, what welcome do we have to offer?

I know, I know, "I am not worthy . . . but only say the word" and all that (Matt 8:8). Guess what? The word has been said. When Jesus said, "As I have loved you, so you should also love one another" (John 13:34), present company was included. If you have been waiting for a day when you have your spiritual house in order, when you have dealt with those "weights and sins which cling so closely" (Heb 12:1), when you are somehow *ready* to accept God's hospitality, stop waiting and start accepting right now. God loves you.

And for heaven's sake don't stop there. This is the start, not the conclusion. The particulars of the practice will vary based on your situation and your personality, but Jesus' instructions were pretty clear: sit in the back, beside the people nobody wants to sit with, and invite to supper those people who need it most but have come to expect it least. Go really, really deep with the practice of hospitality, because it is one of the primary Christian practices. I told one congregation that they could make Charles Manson feel welcome at coffee hour, but they wouldn't invite the Queen of England home for dinner. Of course, our call is to visit those in prison, not those in palaces. What that will look like in your life you will have to tell me. But watch out: there are angels everywhere, just waiting to be entertained.

Chapter Four

Arrangement

In the previous chapters attention has focused on creativity rather than order, knowing that few things frustrate creativity more than order. Good preachers do not prepare sermons by sitting down and typing "Introduction" and banging away at the keyboard until "The End." Good preachers begin with the homiletical question (HQ), explore the biblical texts more deeply, revise the HQ as study and discovery suggest, then develop the "moves" of the sermon—the theological claims that make it possible to gain a hearing for the answer to the HQ—without concern for best ordering of the individual moves. Instead each move is developed as "the Spirit gives utterance" (1 Cor 12:8, RSV).

But a sermon without order is difficult to follow and impossible to remember, so there comes a time when creativity gives way to order, and once that order is established, the preacher may fashion the conclusion and the introduction to the sermon, in that order. In rhetoric this ordering is known as "arrangement," the focus for this chapter.

Theory

Form and content are never far apart. What people hear is an inextricable combination of what one is trying to say and how one goes about saying it. So *structure* may be a better term than *form*. At some point in a guide to liturgical preaching, however, form must be considered because that is the customary term for distinguishing various approaches to the arrangement and direction of a sermon.

A number of elements are part of a preacher's decision about how best to arrange the sermon. Except as an exercise like the one in the section on "practice" below these are never abstract, but are determined by the answer to the HQ. That is, the sermon is structured in the way that will best help gain a hearing for the answer to the HQ for any particular sermon. The preacher who says "I always" before describing her or his way of preparing, arranging, and delivering sermons, has confused preference or habit for faithfulness and effectiveness. It is the answer to the HQ that determines the arrangement of the sermon, and as will be seen in chapter six on style and delivery.

Logic, however, always has its place. A poorly ordered sermon is like a poorly worded sentence—hard to understand. Transitions between moves are important to this logic, but the arrangement of the moves even more so. Teachers of preaching regularly find that the problem with a student's sermon is not the content and development of the individual moves, but the arrangement. What the student thought should come first is more effective later in the sermon, or the dramatic closing move works better as the surprising introduction to the sermon. So, for example, a sermon prepared for the First Sunday of Lent, Year A (Matthew's account of the temptation of Jesus, eating the forbidden fruit in Genesis 3) was being prepared to key on what it means to "see" nakedness—"Then the eyes of both were opened, and they saw that they were naked" (Gen 3:7). The intention was to consider what was lost when Eve and Adam saw "naked" when before they had only seen each other, and the last move was going to begin with "A lot was lost when Adam and Eve discovered 'naked.'" As the sermon was coming together the preacher realized that much would be gained by opening the sermon with this idea, because the answer to the HQ required exploring shame, objectification, body image, etc.—the corruption by our culture of what God had made and declared "good"—and this needed more time. So the sermon began, "'Naked!' That's what God wanted to know. 'Who told you that you were naked?' God asks Adam. 'Since when do you know from naked?'" The change in order had the double advantage of getting everyone's attention and introducing a central claim of the sermon at the start.

Homiletics has and will continue to change its preferences for the form of the sermon and the way it attempts to categorize those preferences, so there is nothing definitive about this attempt. Nor would many homileticians agree that the author is only discussing arrangement/form in this section, and they would be correct, because form and content are inseparable, and homiletical strategy is an important part of any decision about form. Because this is an introductory primer, not a definitive taxonomy of homiletical arrangement/form, the discussion will be limited to the three main types common in liturgical preaching: interpretation-application (deductive), narrative (inductive), and perhaps the most common, a mixed or hybrid form.

Interpretation-application (deductive). Preachers start with texts more times than not, so it is no surprise that their sermons do the same. "In our Gospel reading for today we see . . ." and the preacher launches into a summary of the lesson. Following the summary the preacher then turns to an analogy in contemporary life, and shows how the wisdom of the Gospel helps us know how we ought to live. There are untold variations on this structure depending on preacher, listeners, and occasion. The preacher may treat more than one of the readings for the day, devoting a move to each, demonstrating in conclusion how the collective wisdom of Old Testament, epistle, and Gospel point to a definite course of action, or might argue from another set of readings that one text calls the others into question, so that while multiple texts are interpreted the application to the lives of the listeners is limited to one text. The preacher may also interpret one text verse-by-verse in considerable detail, what has traditionally been termed "expository preaching," finding a point of application to the lives of the listeners in every verse. In most cases the preacher begins by stating a clear, overarching theme that is the goal of the interpretation-application that is developed, or proven, by the exposition. It is more of a "Let me tell you what we find in Scripture" approach than a "Let's take a look and see what we find" approach. Fred B. Craddock famously referred to this as deductive preaching, stating the conclusion at the outset and demonstrating its truth in the development.[1]

The strength of the interpretation-application form is clarity. I agree with Dr. Craddock and others that it is an inherently less interesting way of arranging a sermon, but there are times when clarity is more important than interest. This can be true when an assigned text is obscure, controversial, or complex, be it an Old Testament lesson with a crucial but forgotten historical setting, a miracle or controversy story from a Synoptic Gospel, or an intricate argument by the Apostle Paul. It is also likely that the preacher new to the craft will find the interpretation-application model easier to implement.

1. Craddock, *As One without Authority.*

When one returns to the readings for Lent 1A it is easy to see how this arrangement could be applied to the Gospel text, Matthew 4:1–11. There is an introduction, a conclusion, and three temptations; instant sermon outline. The preacher taking this approach would interpret each of the three temptation scenes—stones into bread, pinnacle of the Temple, nations of the world—and show how something in the lives of the listeners is similar, so that, uh, well, that can be a problem. Because most of the temptations we face are nothing like those Jesus faced. That, admittedly, is an interpretive and homiletical bias, but it is a strong one: not every passage of Scripture is about the reader or listener. Sometime the passage is about Jesus. Period. The important thing is to see how the interpretation-application model would work. So while this author's preference is for inductive preaching, there are admittedly times when a deductive, interpretation-application form is the best choice. Nothing is never and nothing is always in preaching.

In a well-known and important "sermon" by the late Henri Nouwen the temptations of Jesus were compared to the temptations of contemporary ordained ministry. Turning stones into bread was understood as the desire of the pastoral leader to have "relevance." The temptation to fling himself off the pinnacle of the Temple was compared to the desire for "popularity." And the offer of authority over the nations of the world was seen as a temptation to "power."[2] Nouwen's treatment moved back and forth from the episode in the life of Jesus to an argument for a distinctive view of Christian ministry and ministers in a clear, deductive, but effective manner.

Narrative (inductive). While precise definitions of narrative preaching, like those of narrative theology, will differ, for the purpose of this chapter the distinction is primarily of intent and order, in which the logic of the answer to the HQ orders the sermon rather than the logic and/or order of the biblical passage(s). So that although both interpretation-application and narrative models set out to gain a hearing for the answer to the HQ, the narrative model allows the answer to shape the sermon, not the biblical text(s). For many this has become something of an ideology: "I'm a *narrative* preacher." One hopes not; one hopes instead that narrative sermons are preached when that is how best to gain a hearing for the answer to the homiletical question that Sunday. Good preachers are skilled at using multiple forms, depending on what is most effective. Narrative preaching may be a preference, but remember that Jesus did not only tell parables.

---

2. Nouwen, *In the Name of Jesus.*

What does it look like to allow the answer to the HQ to determine the order of the homily? That also depends. Some sermons take the shape of a "V," starting on a high, "The Lord is my shepherd" then falling off a cliff, "Yea though I walk through the valley of the shadow of death," before scaling the heights to a powerful climax, "Surely goodness and mercy will follow me all the days of my life . . . !" Others "start low, go slow, aim higher, light fire!" building every step of the way. Some have surprise endings, others use a repeated phrase or question to reinforce the central theological claim of the sermon.

Return to the First Sunday of Lent, Year A, in particular to Genesis 3, by way of example. A perfectly fine sermon could move through the text and talk about the nature of temptation, the "fall" and so on—in fact that is what the Apostle Paul does in the epistle for the day, Romans 5:12–19. But a sermon could also be grounded in a narrative retelling of the text, not verse by verse but in a more contemporary medium.

> You remember the story. Man and woman in Paradise, all their wants provided for them from the bounty of creation, living naked and unashamed. Enter the talking serpent. Not Satan or the devil or Beelzebub. A talking serpent, who doesn't say, "Heh, heh, heh. Yo, Eve, why don't you have a bite of this magic apple and see what happens?" but craftily asks questions, distorting God's intention and using half-truths to plant doubt and raise possibilities. Eve bites, and shares the delicious, forbidden fruit with Adam. Then all hell breaks loose. God comes by for a stroll in the garden and maybe a glass of sweet tea, but cannot find his walking buddy. When God tracks Adam down, hiding in the hydrangea, Adam mumbles something about having nothing to wear, and my friends, the party is over. From naked and unashamed in Paradise to naked, afraid, and hiding. And God had not said or done a thing. What happened?
>
> My favorite line in the story is "Who told you that you were naked?" What did Adam know from naked? And what a difference it made when he did. Indeed, one of the things our passage suggests is that with sin comes shame, and while the sin may be forgiven somehow the shame lingers on. After all, what can be more natural than naked? Yet naked is shameful. How did that happen? With the loss of innocence comes the discovery of shame, and that strikes me as a sad exchange indeed. Because we project the shame all over creation. It makes us whisper when we need to speak plainly, about, for example, the importance of teaching our children the ways and means to resist casual sexual encounters,

practice safe sex, and avoid unplanned pregnancy. It causes us to project our own insecurities and inhibitions, so that the average married couple never talks about how to enrich their physical intimacy, and a lot of you are getting a little embarrassed that I am even bringing it up. In church. And I'm not done, because the final loss that comes with exchanging shame for innocence is an inability to talk rationally about highly charged questions of human sexuality, for as Bill Countryman and others have taught us, the issue really being discussed is not sexuality but purity codes. When Adam says "naked" he means "impure and unclean." A lot was lost when Adam discovered "naked."

The careful reader will notice that this was, in its own way, interpretation-application, but also that it was not, perhaps because the interpreter was more interested in a particular application than in detailed exegesis.

This example suggests both the complexity and ambiguity of a precise description of narrative preaching, which takes many forms. Rarely, but occasionally, the sermon may be one extended narrative, more often it is a series of interwoven stories, examples, and analogies, with the biblical text(s) in the background, and while often providing the organizing structure of the sermon, the text is not repeatedly cited or explained. Instead it is the dynamic of the biblical narrative driving the dynamic of the sermon. So, for example, while a sermon on the parable of the Good Samaritan may exegete and apply, or might imaginatively retell the story in a modern setting, it could also provide the background of a sermon that explores one or the other of the lawyer's two questions without ever going anywhere near the Jericho road or discussing Samaritans or some supposed modern equivalent.

A further word about "inductive" preaching is helpful here. Craddock famously turned homiletics on its head by suggesting that the conclusion was not the best introduction to the sermon. "Our topic for today is . . . . And so, in conclusion, we find, as I said at the beginning, that . . . ." Doing so removes all tension, most interest, and leaves the listener with little to do beyond trying to stay awake. The preacher of an inductive sermon knows where she or he is going, but does not tell the audience, allowing them the chance to figure that out along the way. Standard issue sermons on the Prodigal Son will focus on God's forgiving love as depicted in the character of the father. An inductive sermon might start, "'A man had two sons,' Jesus begins this story. Later in the Creed we will say that Jesus is 'The only son of the father.' So I guess this parable is not about God. I wonder who it is about?" Only in the last move will the listeners learn that the story is about their own call to be always forgiving. Deductive preaching proves a thesis. Inductive preaching arrives at a conclusion. Both can use narrative, but usually it is the inductive sermon.

Mixed or hybrid forms. Pure examples exist in theory much more so than in practice. So what many preach most of the time is a sermon that is part interpretation-application, part narrative. And that is just fine. Moreover, the type of arrangement/form giving shape to the sermon is rarely planned from the outset, and is instead recognized after the fact. If a student is asked what was the model of arrangement used in shaping the sermon the response is usually "Huh?" The instructor may write in the critique that the sermon was an excellent example of a narrative inductive sermon, and the student will be completely surprised. Intentionally varying sermon form between deductive and inductive, and experimenting with variations in the use of person, voice, and style, comes later. So long as the arrangement of the sermon is determined by the answer to the HQ, mixed forms are more than fine.

Propositional, thematic, or doctrinal sermons often take a mixed form because explanation is at the heart of sermon's purpose—what the Holy Spirit wants the people of God to hear on Trinity Sunday, for example, is a coherent explanation of the Holy Trinity. Here one might point out the relative absence of Trinitarian language in Scripture, usually well-evidenced in readings for the day, then offer a historical or theological example to demonstrate why and how the tradition began to find such language crucial to understanding the faith. In conclusion, however, the preacher turns to a story that helps Trinitarian language become alive and accessible. The reverse is also common: a sermon with a strong narrative trajectory will devote one move to biblical exposition. To the extent one might consider portions of Paul's letters to be a type of "sermon" one finds him regularly using a mixed or hybrid form, alternating biblical and theological exposition with metaphor and analogy.

Individual moves are shaped by the logic of the move. The arrangement of those moves is determined by the logic of the sermon, i.e., where the Holy Spirit wants the sermon to go, and how the preacher has decided is the best way to get there. For example, one is preaching on the Third Sunday of Epiphany, Year B, and the Revised Common Lectionary texts are from Jonah (the repentance of the people of Nineveh, 3:1–5, 10), Psalm 62 ("For God alone my soul in silence waits"), a snippet of 1 Corinthians

(7:29–31, "the present form of this world is passing away"), and Jesus' first proclamation of the kingdom and the call of four disciples in Mark 1:14–20. Racing through the first half of sermon preparation it seems that the Holy Spirit wants the people of God to focus on how to respond to God's call right here, right now. Possible moves include:

1. Paul advises the Corinthians to remain as they are because the kingdom is coming right now, much as Jesus says the kingdom is "at hand." Were they right or wrong?

2. Jonah calls for repentance, and much to his surprise and chagrin, that is what the people of Nineveh do. What does it mean to repent? What does it look like?

3. In Jonah 3 it is God who "changed his mind" (i.e., repented); what does that mean?

4. The four disciples drop everything and leave family behind to "fish for people," a fairly ridiculous metaphor for evangelization when you stop and think about it. (I would rather be a lost sheep than a fish in a net, if those are my choices.)

5. The psalmist says "wait."

6. What does it mean for the listeners to respond to God's call—repent, drop everything: go and follow, wait, something else?

One preacher decides that this combination of very brief passages allows focused attention on each one, and plans an interpretation-application sermon that moves through each passage after an introduction that announces that "There is no right way to respond to the call of God. In different times, different lives, God's call is different. What matters is that we respond. If we look briefly at our lessons for today I think you will see what I mean."

Another preacher decides that she is more or less after the same goal, but will only allude to the lessons while telling a series of stories about the various ways people in a community like theirs have heard and responded to God's call. She will conclude, "I do not know what God is calling you to do right now. Heck, most of the time I am not sure what God is calling *me* to do. But the call is for here and now. We did not miss it, and it is not far, far away. Perhaps, just perhaps, if we learn how to sit with the psalmist, and give our souls space to wait in silence, we will hear it."

A third preacher feels called to wrestle with the question of whether Paul and Jesus were right or wrong to proclaim the imminent arrival of the kingdom. What does it mean to declare that "the time is fulfilled and the kingdom of God has come near"? She plans to start with the responses of the Ninevites and the four disciples, who all "drop everything," and explore what her parish may be called on to "drop" in order to faithfully follow in this critical time.

A fourth preacher, who has retained a little biblical Hebrew and Greek, is fascinated by the terminology of repentance, and in particular by the idea that in the book of Jonah, God, in the King James Version, "repented of the evil that he had said he would do unto them, and he did it not" (Jonah 3:10). This preacher is planning a sermon on the meaning of repentance, finding biblical and historical examples to illustrate the meaning of the terms and idea before asking the listeners to examine their own lives, and consider sharing in the "rite of reconciliation." More time will be given at the confession so that all may wait in silence for the Lord.

The possibilities are not endless, but they are indeed numerous. As said before there is only one homiletical question, but each Sunday there are thousands of "right" answers.

Practice

While it may not suit every preacher, the freedom to work on the sermon without worry about the final sequence is liberating for most. Moves can be developed independent of concern for sequence, and the conclusion and introduction postponed until such time as the preacher knows what it is she or he will be introducing, and how to fashion a conclusion that recapitulates and sharply focuses the theme of the sermon. There are multiple models for arranging the sermon, depending on the answer to the HQ and how the preacher determines that answer may best be heard on the occasion at hand. This section plays with possible arrangements of a homily on the readings for the 22nd Sunday after Pentecost, Year A, Proper 28. For simplicity's sake the readings are from Revised Common Lectionary Track 2: Zephaniah 1:7, 12–18; Psalm 90; 1 Thessalonians 5:1–11 and Matthew 25:14–30.

The Gospel is the parable of the Talents, and most preachers would agree it is difficult to ignore a reading of such magnitude and length. The epistle is something of an eschatological mishmash, with a thief in the night, labor pains, admonishment to be sober and awake, a few pieces of the armor of righteousness, and this verse which catches the preacher's attention:

"For God has destined us not for wrath but for obtaining salvation through our Lord Jesus Christ" (1 Thess 5:9). Zephaniah is full-blown prophetic terror. "In the fire of his passion the whole earth shall be consumed; for a full, a terrible end he will make of all the inhabitants of the earth" (Zeph 1:18), which Psalm 90 softens a bit while still encouraging us to "number our days."

One preacher, having concluded that the Holy Spirit wants the people of God to learn about the parable, decides to keep the prophet and the apostle in the background, offering an extra bit of eschatological urgency should that seem needed, and devotes attention almost exclusively to the parable. The following moves emerge:

1. Matthew 25 is the last of Jesus' five "sermons" in the gospel, and the last teaching before the Passion. It must therefore be uniquely important.

2. Zephaniah and Paul are both expecting the "day of the Lord" but one could hardly say they were "waiting"—they expected it yesterday.

3. The parable of the talents is primarily a story of lost opportunities. The third servant, paralyzed by fear ("I knew you were a harsh man"), stashes the money where it will at least be safe from theft or confiscation.

4. People of faith must be willing to take risks for the kingdom, and make investments in the gospel, if they wish to hear "Well done, good and trustworthy slave" on judgment day.

The sermon that emerges is straight interpretation-application, one step at a time, leading to a call for setting aside our fears and responding boldly to the good news of Jesus Christ.

1. Move One: The day of the Lord. Interpretation: The prophet Zephaniah and the Apostle Paul each expected the coming of the Lord to be a "great and terrible day," and were convinced it was right around the corner. Application: You may have seen the billboard or bumper sticker that says, "If you were to die tomorrow, where would you go?" We should each ask ourselves that question every day.

2. Move Two: The parable of the talents. Interpretation: The preacher offers a rehearsal of the story, pointing out how common absentee landlords were in the ancient Mediterranean world, the significance of the amount of money involved, and other interesting and important facts.

Application: Our world is not as different from the world of the parable as we might think. We all have obligations, rarely see the person who signs our paychecks, etc.

3. Move Three: The third servant. Interpretation: The preacher returns to the character of the third servant, explains his actions, and suggests that he was likely surprised at the harsh judgment. Application: The third servant was paralyzed by his fear, which caused him to misunderstand what was at stake, so that his caution became the source of his ruin. What are we afraid of? Where are we too cautious?

4. Move Four: Our challenge. The last move begins with some recapitulation, but is almost all application, telling the story of a person who set aside her fears and became a great athlete, musician, physician, missionary—the details are not important, because the stress is on not being paralyzed by fear, and instead living by faith. If we too set aside our fears and trust in God's grace, we can also do great things. If we do not, we may lose what little we have.

Another preacher prepared a sermon on the same readings but could not shake the image of the third servant. His fears were justified, his treatment harsh and undeserved, just like the treatment of the five foolish maidens in the story just before, Matthew 25:1–13. The Holy Spirit was guiding this preacher to ask and answer a different set of questions, to help the listeners understand what it means to be excluded, to be condemned, to be forced to live in the "outer darkness" on the wrong side of the closed and locked door. Because the preacher knows that when the listeners are honest with themselves they have to admit that the doors have always been open to them, and if they were not the one handing out the talents, they certainly knew how to double their money. The preacher was called to foster understanding and compassion for those who were falling behind, underwater, and struggling to make ends meet. A more or less seamless narrative sermon emerged, offered mostly in the second person, after an introduction inviting the listeners into the world of the parable, but entirely from the perspective of the third servant, who is referred to as "you" in order to foster strong identification between the listeners and the third servant. The sermon begins with, "It is not your dream job, but in this economy you are happy to have any job at all. There are hardly any benefits, and no job security, but you make enough to get by. Someday soon, you pray, something better will come along. Until then you do what you are told, and try to not call too much attention to yourself." The sermon did not end on an upbeat note. The Prayers of the People stressed the needs of the poor and the oppressed, those sick and in prison, and the offertory sentence was taken from Matthew 11, "Come unto me all you that are weary and heavy laden, and I will give you rest."

A third sermon was crafted as a mixed form, with some exegesis, but more reading against the texts, or more accurately, reading against traditional readings (and preaching) on the texts. The preacher was intrigued by the tradition's focus on the third servant, the foolish virgins, and the "goats" in Matthew 25, and by Paul's almost throwaway line noted earlier, "For God has destined us not for wrath but for obtaining salvation through our Lord Jesus Christ." The sermon starts with the theme of judgment in biblical and cultural contexts (move one) then asks why do we hear the word *judgment* as if it always means *condemnation* (move two). The sermon then looks at the stories of Matthew 25 in a different light (move three) and concludes by offering simple stories of the small things that are the measure of our faith (move four). This sermon, in its entirety, now follows.

Sermon for the 22nd Sunday after Pentecost, Year A, Proper 28

What is the measure of your faith? Our readings today, and the larger biblical context from which the readings emerge, suggest different, though complementary, answers.

We do not know a great deal about Zephaniah, though it appears he was probably one of the early organizers of a movement to "Occupy Jerusalem." He seems an angry fellow, likely carrying a Hebrew version of the signs I saw on television the other night, "Taxidermy the rich" and "Kill the bastards before they kill us." The measure of faith for Zephaniah was resistance to idolatry, and trust in God rather than trust in wealth or might.

What is the measure of your faith?

Paul, at least in this early conversation with the Thessalonians, also thought the measure of faith was trust in God. He shared with Zephaniah an expectation of the imminent "Day of the Lord," and for what it's worth ruined sermons about the difference between *chronos* and *kairos* in the first verse ("Now concerning the *times* and the *seasons*, brothers and sisters, you do not need to have anything written to you") so please don't bother. Paul's emphasis was on hope, hope in the promise of resurrection.

What is the measure of your faith?

Jesus, in Matthew 25, shares the prophet's and the apostle's eschatological focus, but with his own distinctive twist. He tells three stories, and the twist, which many parable scholars see as at least as much indebted to Matthew as to Jesus, is how a time of delay figures into the stories. The measure of faith then becomes what one does in anticipation of and during the delay, because at the final *dénouement* there is no room for excuse or explanation. The question, which apparently cannot be begged, is what do we understand to be the measure of our faith?

Sharing another liturgy with Matthew means sharing in his considerable interest in eschatological judgment. We might as well get used to it because it is not going to get any better in Advent when we trade Matthew's Jesus for Mark's John the Baptist. There is a significant disconnect between tradition and practice here. The Bible speaks of judgment, the Day of the Lord, and the consequences of sin on a regular basis, our texts today a representative sample, not three outliers. The sermons, pamphlets, books, and teachings of our Anglican, Methodist, and Catholic forbearers shared this focus on judgment. Our sermons? Not so much. And that is a problem.

I think Rob Bell is correct, *Love Wins*, but love and justice, we are told and ourselves often say, are not opposites. Love requires justice, discernment, and decision, makes distinctions and yes, even separates sheep and goats. So why do we find it so difficult to talk honestly about judgment, doomsday books, days of the Lord, and Matthew's beloved weeping and gnashing of teeth place?

Preachers tell me that they do not want to drive people away, and talk of judgment is negative and off-putting. They want to proclaim the *luuvv* of God. Who doesn't? But I do not trust the "I don't want to talk about judgment because it is depressing" explanation. Why? Like you I look in the mirror most mornings, and even if it is a glass darkly I remember what I see, and what I see is someone who doesn't preach about judgment because that shoe fits too well. Which brings us to Jesus.

Jesus, especially Jesus in Matthew, talks about judgment all the time, in all its eschatological if not apocalyptic glory. Jesus tells three complementary, almost interwoven, stories of judgment in Matthew 25. Our text, the story of the talents, comes in the middle of the series, and the chapter as a whole comes at the end of three chapters of unremitting judgment admittedly replete with condemnation. The scribes and the Pharisees come first in a series of seven "woes" in chapter 23, then everyone else gets theirs in the description of the fall of Jerusalem in chapter 24. So far Matthew is following the same script as Mark and Luke, but chapter 25 is all his own, three extended narrative depictions of what the previous chapters outline.

The stories share focus on the decisive moment of judgment, and on the distribution of characters into those who are welcomed at the end of the story and those who are excluded. Significantly, the basis for inclusion/exclusion is not theological conviction, biblical hermeneutic, or SAT scores. The first story affirms the adage usually attributed to Woody Allen, "Eighty percent of success is just showing up." The second and third stories suggest that the other 20 percent is about what we do when we get there. But if I asked you what you remember from these stories my guess is that most of you would say:

1. The foolish virgins arrive to find the door locked and the bridegroom saying, "I do not know you."

2. The master says to the one talent guy, "You wicked slave," takes the talent away, and casts him into the weeping/gnashing place.

3. The king says to the goats, "Depart from me into the eternal fire prepared for the devil and his angels."

I suppose it makes sense that when reading passages with eschatological emphasis that we expect and highlight end stress. So we focus our interpretive and homiletical energy on those not welcomed to the banquet, the one not praised, and those condemned for what they failed to do. But that is only half of the stories, and in the case of the talents, only a third of the story. Why is it so hard to see the hope and promise in these stories?

Almost every sermon I have ever preached and you have ever heard on the stories in Matthew 25 spent most of its time on the one talent servant, the foolish virgins, and the goats. Why is it so difficult to focus on, "Well done, good and faithful slave . . . enter into the joy of your master"? Is it just our guilty consciences that cause us to think "condemnation" when someone says "judgment day"? I know the portion of Psalm 90 we read was pretty bleak, but the rest is almost upbeat. "Satisfy us by your loving-kindness in the morning; so shall we rejoice and be glad all the days of our life" (v. 14, Book of Common Prayer). The Apostle Paul reminds the Thessalonians, "God has destined us not for wrath but for obtaining salvation . . . ." The fact is that two of the slaves are praised, and one is condemned. If we choose to focus on condemnation and not salvation in this story that says something about the measure of our faith, not the measure at work in the story.

The "good and faithful slave" has been "faithful in small things" and so shall be responsible for many. The measure of faith is not the grandeur of our accomplishments or the depth and breadth of our *oeuvre*. In these stories it is how we have handled the *oligos*, the small stuff.

What most people will remember from the consecration of Mariann Budde as the ninth bishop of Washington, DC is not the pageantry, the drumming and pomp and splendor, but Bishop Katharine's insistence on holding the silence at the prayer of consecration long past our collective discomfort into a true invocation of the Spirit, and how beautifully the new bishop's sons chanted the litany for ordination in English and Spanish. Stunning, the small stuff.

When in years to come the School of Theology in Sewanee recalls its deep debt to Dean William Stafford it will remember the health restored to the School, the new programs, and the foundation for the future, but above all it will remember how its way of looking at the world was changed by the example Bill and his wife Barbara gave in welcoming their adopted children Jasmine and David into their lives, and the life of the community.

We know that ministry *is* in the interruptions, that God, and not the devil, is in the details, and that our capacity to make a difference in the lives of others is limited only by our willingness to care. We call these truisms because they are true. To keep us on our toes Jesus sometimes suggests that we move mountains, give up our possessions, or feed a multitude, things so great they seem impossible, and we, like the ruler with many possessions, turn away sadly. Pray God we might have the measure of faith to realize it does not happen all at once, we are not called to do it alone, and that it is over a lifetime of faithfulness in small things that great things are indeed possible, with and through the one in whom all things truly are.

Chapter Five

Introductions and Conclusions

Linus is walking out of the room in an old *Peanuts* cartoon. Sister Lucy points out that he shined only the front of his shoes. "I don't care what people think of me when I'm leaving." That, alas, is all too often true of sermons. The preacher puts plenty of time, energy, and creativity into the introduction, hoping to capture the listeners' attention in the few moments at the beginning of the sermon when they think that is possible, but having run out of preparation time, then settles for a string of clichés in closing. Why is that, and what can a good preacher do about it? To begin, understand the important functions of conclusions and introductions, and prepare accordingly.

Conclusions

Theory

It may seem odd to begin the chapter with conclusions, but in fact the last thing a good preacher prepares is the introduction, for only after the body and ending of the sermon have been crafted does the preacher know what it is she or he is trying to introduce. So the chapter starts with conclusions, with a nod toward the late Steven Covey's first habit of highly effective people: begin with the end in mind.[1] To put it practically, where is the sermon headed? What is the impact the preacher intends, what does the preacher hope the listeners will think, believe and do because they heard this particular sermon? To put it homiletically, what does the Holy Spirit want the

---

1. Covey, *The Seven Habits of Highly Effective People.*

people of God to hear from these texts on this occasion? The conclusion is the last chance the preacher has to help that happen; after the sermon the liturgy will do the rest.

The conclusion to the sermon usually has three functions: to reiterate the answer to the HQ; to provide a vivid, concrete, and specific example of what the preacher prays the listeners will think, believe and do in response to the sermon; and to offer a rhetorically effective moment of inspiration that "leaves" the listeners where the preacher has concluded the Holy Spirit wants them to be. All of this is rhetorically indistinguishable from what has come before. The preacher will use similar words, images, style, and delivery. Having invested eight to ten minutes or more in introducing and developing the answer to the HQ, the conclusion is no time to veer in another direction.

The conclusion reiterates the answer to the HQ in a variety of ways. If the sermon is deductive the preacher will begin the conclusion with something like, "We have seen, therefore, that the outrageous suggestion with which I began this sermon is true: God does not 'hate the sin but loves the sinner,' God loves the sinner and *forgives* the sin. There is no hate in God." Deductive sermons are fond of "therefore." Inductive sermons, however (a favorite inductive term), may state the answer to the HQ for the first time in the conclusion. The sermon has been building up to it, circling around it, suggesting it but not claiming it directly until the last turn of the page. "How incredible it is to realize, perhaps for the first time, that there is no hate in God. God is love." Reiteration is not recapitulation or summarization, but restating, saying again in mostly similar but still slightly different words. The conclusion is not the time to introduce new ideas, terms, or speech patterns, but gives the preacher a chance to reinforce the claim(s) already made. So, for example, a sermon on 1 John 4 ("God is love") may begin the conclusion with, "Augustine said, 'Love God and do what you want.' That is one sentence. Not, 'Love God. (Pause.) Do what you want.' He believed that when you love God you can do what you want because what you want and what God wants are pretty much the same."

The conclusion provides a final image that offers a vivid, concrete, and specific example of the behavior the preacher hopes the listeners will emulate. The absence of such examples is one of the greatest single failings of far too many sermons. Preachers inspire their listeners, they are moved and motivated to take action, but they are not quite sure what it is they are being asked to do. They need to see one more time what it would look like to act in the way the sermon invites them to. Far too frequently the preacher instead provides vague exhortations and generic "shoulds" when the listener is thinking, "I really like your idea of 'living into' my faith; can you show me what that would look like because I am pretty short on examples in my own life?"

So the preacher might say, "Living into the faith, hope and love of God is a lot more like climbing a mountain than it is like jumping off a cliff. I really don't know why we talk about a 'leap of faith.' It is more one step after another, at times sideways, sometimes sliding back. We only take the picture when we arrive at the summit, but every step is needed to get there." Four short sentences, suggesting an approach to the life of faith without prescribing it. The preacher could provide an added instance or two of what this manner of "living into" feels like, but it may not be necessary.

Finally, the conclusion provides an added rhetorical "oomph." At least that is the technical term. This may be a matter of delivery, the voice raised or lowered dramatically, an extended pause, the recitation of the key biblical passage or a line from a poem. It may be borrowed, created, or a final bit of reiteration. But like everything else it is a part of the answer to the HQ and consonant with the whole of the sermon and the person of the preacher. And as will be seen in a section on "do's and don'ts" below, there is no one best way to bring the sermon to a conclusion. In fact the last thing a good preacher does is end each sermon the same way.

In the sermon preparation process the conclusion is kept in mind throughout, but it is not developed until after the main moves of the sermon have been sketched, crafted, and arranged. One of three things generally occurs at this point in the process. (1) The conclusion follows with relative ease; (2) the preacher attempts to craft a conclusion that solves a problem created by one of the moves or the arrangement of the moves; or (3) the preacher admits there is a problem, that it cannot be magically be solved in a 90–120 second conclusion, and returns to working on the moves. Good conclusions do not rescue bad sermons.

The dynamic of the conclusion must follow, not subvert, the dynamic of the rest of the sermon. Only rarely should a sermon have a "surprise ending." While the comparison is often made (*mea culpa*), even inductive sermons are not murder mysteries. A dramatic sermon will have a dramatic conclusion, a first-person monologue will stay in character, not use the conclusion to say, "So what did we learn from our 'visit' by the Apostle Peter today?" A playful sermon should have a light ending, not a sudden,

"But as we all know, life is not so easy." If the preacher is ironic or skeptical through most of the sermon, the conclusion is not the time to get syrupy and sincere.

The conclusion is also not an occasion for closure, bringing the sermon full circle, or tying up all the loose ends. Sometimes, perhaps, but nothing is never and nothing is always in preaching, and our worship is not over with the sermon. In tangible if often indirect ways the sermon anticipates and points to prayers, offering, and Eucharist. There is also next week. Not every problem imagined in the homily for this week is resolved this week. Some things, like grace, forgiveness, hope, love, redemption—okay, most things—take more time than is available for this homily. Which does not mean one creates artificial cliffhangers—"If you want to know what Jesus really meant you will have to come back next Sunday." Nor does one artificially avoid closure by ending the sermon with a rhetorical question. For as often as it is used, the rhetorical question is in fact almost always a very weak ending, and good preachers find more effective ways to leave the audience reflecting on what the sermon calls for than asking, "And so, I ask, what will *you* do?" and making a dramatic turn away from the pulpit. It is fun, absolutely, to "drop the mike." But it is also a kind of homiletical hot-dogging, like the batter who stares at flight of the ball anticipating the dramatic "walk-off" home run. Most times the ball never clears the fence.

Practice

In theory, one might give an able preacher the introduction and body of a sermon and ask him or her to provide a compelling conclusion. So much for theory: this was tried once in a workshop and it failed miserably, for reasons that in hindsight should have bene clear from the previous discussion. If an effective conclusion is all of a piece with the body of the sermon, its conclusion cannot come from just any preacher, but has to come from the preacher who crafted the rest of the sermon. So, like more or less all of the "practice" sections in this book, what follows is contrived, only possibly even a little more so. (As in prior chapters, these are actual examples from real sermons. No listeners were injured in testing this material.)

The first example comes from a text that Sunday preachers should fear more than they do, Lent 4C, with all twenty-one verses of the parable of the Prodigal Son and a three-verse introduction from the start of Luke 15 providing one of the longer Gospel readings in the lectionary. Time is in short supply, and the sense of "been there, heard that" fills the church. The preacher has taken the "everything you may have heard about this parable is wrong" approach, because, to be honest, it probably is. In particular the preacher challenges the allegorical reading of the story that assumes the father is God, the listeners are the wayward son, and the Pharisees/the vestry/the establishment is the older son. Why, the sermon begins, would one want to be compared to the younger son? He's a jerk. The core argument is that the listener, the church, is called to be like the father, waiting, watching, welcoming and forgiving, then also going out to the angry other child, because joy is not in being found . . .

> The joy is in the finding. I cannot tell you how important that phrase is. We are culturally programmed to think that the joy is in being found, and it is, to an extent. But folks who spend their lives lurching from disaster to disaster, always waiting for someone to come and save them, are usually considered immature and self-destructive. Yes, we do need to be "saved," but it is theologically considered to be a once-for-life experience—"I once was lost / but now I'm found." Now you're found. Okay, then what happens? Get lost again so you can be "saved" again? Or become a seeker and saver of the lost?
>
> This is just as true of the church as it is of the Christian. Joy is not in sitting together, comparing notes on our relative degree of "foundness." Joy is in reaching out to the lost, reaching out in every way imaginable—from Habitat houses to mission trips, from hospice and Alzheimer's respite care to church camp, from "Bibles and Brewskis" Bible studies to supporting struggling parishes in the diocese; in anything and everything: the joy is in the finding.
>
> You know what a prodigal is? A prodigal isn't someone who squanders a father's money with impunity. That's a teenager. A prodigal is someone who spends good money after bad, never counting the cost. The prodigal in this story is the father, not the younger son. The prodigal in our lives and faith is God, who never stops giving. You want to have more joy in your life? Be a giver, a seeker, a prodigal. The joy is in the finding.

A fair argument can be made that the conclusion proper begins with "You know what a prodigal is?" and the paragraphs before are the last move. That may be correct, and whether the conclusion is a move is a matter of terminology. This example was chosen to illustrate reiteration, example, and vivid language ("That's a teenager").

The second example comes from later in Year B, the Sixth Sunday after Easter, John 15, "Greater love has no one than this, to lay down one's life for ones friends." The preacher notes that the author of the Fourth Gospel has deliberately chosen not to say, "die for our friends" but "lay down one's life for ones friends." Completely different verbs with completely different semantic fields and ranges of meaning. So the preacher, in a sermon on Mother's Day (that's an occasion), concludes, Greater love has no one than this—to stop putting themselves first.

> We have all of us experienced the truth of this in our lives, to greater or lesser degrees, because from time to time we actually do put someone else first, and because we have had others put us ahead of themselves. Incredible feeling, isn't it, to love and be loved? Jesus was reminding us of that. How blessed are those of us who have mothers who put us first, but not all the time; who remember to care for themselves, and to teach us how to both take care of ourselves and to remember that it is not always about us. Oh the stories we could tell.
>
> Your "friends," your "loved ones," are not anonymous some-ones on the other side of somewhere. They are the people you live with, work with, and worship with. We usually need to bump into the "others" before we can "do unto them" anything much worth mentioning. What have you laid down for your friends? What have you let go of so that others might take it up for themselves? We are, all of us, pretty much always looking for love. Funny thing. You know where we find the love we are looking for? We find it wherever we give it.

In this conclusion the preacher used a dynamic, "laying down" as letting go, and employs an undetailed example of a mother who does what the preacher is calling for. The listeners will have to fill in the blanks for themselves.

Finally in this section, consider a sermon for the Second Sunday of Advent, Year A. Paul is quoting Isaiah in Romans 15, John the Baptist is being full bore John the Baptist in Matthew 3, and Isaiah is imagining how things will be different "on that day" in chapter 11, which begins,

> A shoot shall come out from the stump of Jesse, / and a branch shall grow out of his roots. / The spirit of the LORD shall rest on him, / the spirit of wisdom and understanding, / the spirit of counsel and might, / the spirit of knowledge and the fear of the LORD.

The Holy Spirit wanted the people of God to imagine how things, many things, could be different—in the world, their town and parish, their own lives. The preacher used a scene from the 1947 classic *Miracle on 34th Street* ("You've heard of the French nation and the German nation, well this is the *imagi*-nation") and the idea of the biblical authors' eschatological imaginations to challenge the ecclesial tendency to think that nothing ever changes and if it does it changes for the worst. The sermon concludes,

> So, Christian, it will need to be Isaiah's imagination that guides us this Advent, teaching us how to learn peace, beginning in Jerusalem, and all Judea and Samaria, even to the ends of the earth. What does that look like? You'll have to use your imagination. Not make believe, not wishing so that it will be so, but imagining God's dream for creation, and for your little corner in it. Then imagining what you need to do to get from here to there, and taking those steps.
>
> We usually fail, I think, not for lack of faith and trust and effort, but because we lack the imagination to see how things could be different. Isaiah imagined peace. "They will not hurt or destroy on all my holy mountain." Peace. In Jerusalem. Crazy. Seriously, seriously crazy. *Glory to God, whose power working in us can do infinitely more than we can ask or imagine.* Crazy.

"In conclusion"—never say that. Neither transition to the conclusion by asking, "So what does this mean for us today?" which is the same as saying, "Now you can start listening; everything before was rubbish." Good preaching ends in a way consonant with what came before, restates the answer to the HQ, and anticipates both the rest of the liturgy and the call on the community in the days to come. That is a lot to do in a short paragraph or two, which is another reason that good preachers budget time for developing conclusions as part of their preparation process.

Introductions

Theory

The last step in sermon crafting is the introduction. Period. No excuses, no "they will really love this story so I'll start with it next Sunday," no "I always like to open with a joke" nonsense. "A funny thing happened to me on the way to the pulpit." Really? Every week? The rules for introductions are not unlike those for conclusions: introductions are the first opportunity to introduce the answer to the HQ, so the introduction must be specific to the sermon for the day; introductions should be concise and vivid; introductions should flow naturally into the first move of the sermon.

While there are of course exceptions, especially for the guest preacher, as a rule there is no need to clutter the introduction with greetings, glad-to-be-here's and good-to-see-you's. They know. Nor can a preacher turn to some "joke book" or "1001 great intros." Augustine said "profit with delight," not "yucks and patter." We may learn from them, but preachers are not comedians (from whom we learn timing), actors (emotional range), or entertainers (interactive communication). Nor, in a liturgical tradition, is there reason to offer a public prayer or a bowdlerized Scripture verse (let the words of *my* mouth and the meditations of *our* hearts is not how Psalm 19:14 reads), although there is great wisdom in praying quietly during the sequence hymn.

David Buttrick wisely points out that if the introduction is to the occasion, or to the idea of preaching in general, then a second introduction to the sermon being preached that day will be necessary.[2] Good preachers weave occasion into the introduction, because it is a part of the answer to the HQ. So a sermon at a baptism that intends to focus especially on baptism will not start talking about how difficult the texts for the day are and then careen across Scripture and liturgy to say, "But never mind that, we are here for a baptism." Preliminary remarks do not introduce the sermon, they delay the sermon.

Good introductions, while having in mind the sermon that is beginning to unfold in answer to the HQ, are nevertheless vivid and concise. Concise and vivid go together. Long-winded may have started out vivid, but three minutes in has been replaced by tedious, and all is lost. There is discussion among homileticians about how long preachers have before the listeners decide whether the sermon is going to be about something of importance to them. Some years ago Frederick Buechner said it was three minutes, but now it is probably only a moment or two.[3] In any event it is not long, and the challenge is not to announce, "I have decided to preach on a topic of great importance to each person in this church," but to introduce the answer to the HQ in such a way that the listeners decide, "Hey, this might be important." The sermon on the occasion of a baptism might begin, "We have been waiting months, haven't we, to baptize Alyssa, Frederick, and Antonia. This time last year we were praying for and with their

2. Buttrick, *Homiletic*, 83.
3. Buechner, *Telling the Truth*.

mothers during their pregnancies, then prayed in joy and thanksgiving at the news of their births. Now they are so *big*! Why the delay until Epiphany, some asked, when the babies might catch cold, for heaven's sake? That's it, of course. For *heaven's* sake." Many preachers I know might save this for the conclusion, as a segue to the next moment in the liturgy, but it is better as an introduction, particularly for a sermon that wants to focus theologically on baptism.

Vivid is tricky, and not the starting point in developing the introduction. Preachers should not be pacing the floor wondering what will "grab" their listeners' attention. That leads not to introductions but to irrelevant or tangential ideas and images which then require a transition to the actual introduction. Instead vivid is a part of the language and the intention of the preacher in service of the answer to the HQ. A sermon on 1 Corinthians 13 began, "I gave Paul up for Lent. I know, where's the sacrifice in that?" A lot is going on in those two sentences, and the listeners *really* wanted to know where it was going to go. Capturing their attention in a way that fires their imaginations is the idea, but not by being farfetched or so disconnected from the readings that the question is, "I wonder how we are supposed to make sense of that?"

Which is why the third element of a good introduction is that it flows naturally to the first move of the sermon. The sermon on 1 Corinthians 13 moved from how Paul can drive us crazy to how impoverished our faith would be without him, warts and all. The sermon on baptism moved to the idea that baptism was too important to casually toss into any and every liturgy, important enough to wait for. This is much easier to do when the preacher knows what the first move of the sermon is going to be. Transitions are always easier to craft in reverse, a bridge between two known sets of ideas and images.

The "rules" for introductions are therefore few, but important. (1) The introduction is crafted after all the other elements of the sermon are in place so that (2) it is an introduction to the actual sermon and (3) is vivid and interesting in service of the answer to the HQ and not merely for the sake of being memorable and then (4) transitions smoothly to the first move of the sermon. For the most part this universally excludes jokes, amusing anecdotes, complaints about the readings, and anything that might begin with, "I just have to tell you about . . . ."

Practice

Let's start with a bad example, a sermon for Trinity Sunday, Year B; Moses and the "burning bush" from Exodus 3 and Nicodemus and Jesus from John 3. The preacher has concluded that the Holy Spirit wants the people of God to reflect on the place of mystery in their lives, and so begins,

> Scripture is filled with mystery. The mystery of creation is a fascinating place to start—the Spirit of God "brooding over the face of the deep." How to understand the differing accounts of Genesis 1 and 2, and how to relate those accounts to what contemporary astrophysicists, paleontologists, geologists, and a host of other scientists tell us about the origin of the universe and of life on earth involves serious and searching questions. And, to my mind, also involves mystery.
>
> From the creation of the cosmos through the history of Israel to the incarnation, from the paschal mystery to the gift of the Spirit, the promise of the resurrection and on to the final mysteries of the eschaton, Scripture is shot through with mystery. And we hate it, or at least many of us do. We don't want mystery, we want doctrine. Questions demand answers, clear, precise, and eternal answers.
>
> So we try to "resolve" the mysteries of our faith, insisting that one must choose between "creation" and "evolution," for example, though, interestingly, those who insist on such choices never seem to insist that we choose between the account of creation found in Genesis 1 over against the vastly different account in Genesis 2, or vice versa. But that is a sermon for another time.
>
> Today we meet in our lessons two clear mysteries, one to Moses and one to Nicodemus, and this time I do want you to choose—who are you most like?

Embarrassing, isn't it? Two hundred words of introduction to the generic idea of mystery, which was confused with uncertainty, and ended with, "But that is a sermon for another time." Ouch. The only thing I can say in my defense is, um, nothing.

A better example comes from a sermon for the Second Sunday of Advent, Year C; more John the Baptist and Malachi, called upon and calling the listeners to "prepare the way of the Lord." The preacher had over the years given many Advent sermons focused on John the Baptist and decided to look back and see how he had done, and was distressed to see how often the point had been missed. The temptation is to read the Gospels solely thrrough the occasion, Advent, so completely that the gospel is misread. Imagining that he was not alone, the preacher explored what would happen if the HQ was asked instead of beginning with, "Not John the Baptist again!"

> Prepare the way of the Lord. You've heard this sermon before, right? The preacher talks about decorations and presents and cookies and cards, and then says we must not only make preparations for the coming of Christmas but also prepare our hearts for the coming of the Lord. Sound familiar? I've preached it; you've heard it; and there is nothing wrong with it. Except when we read the Gospel lesson where "Prepare the way" is found, and the passage from Isaiah on which the Gospel lesson is based, we find that Christmas decorations and open hearts are not the subject. "Prepare the way of the Lord." Not make preparations for Christmas, not even prepare your hearts for the coming of the baby Jesus. "Prepare ye the way of the Lord." Second person plural imperative. Y'all. A command. Prepare ye the way of the Lord. And who do you suppose the "Ye" is? Y'all. Not, "Be prepared." That's the Boy Scouts. Prepare.

This introduction is a variation on "everything you have ever heard about John the Baptist is probably wrong," and notice that while the preacher mentioned his culpability ("I've preached it") he did not dwell on it. The sermon moved quickly to the new reading for that particular Sunday, and transitioned into the first move with, "How in heaven are we supposed to prepare the Lord's way? We are not in the mountain-leveling, valley-exalting business. Road building and way-preparing are not in our job description. We don't do infrastructure." The sermon then moved to considering what preparing the Lord's way could look like in the lives of the listeners and the life of the parish.

Finally for this section, before moving to a few very specific opinions of the author on what to do and what to avoid in crafting conclusions and introductions, an example from more than a few years ago. The cultural references are dated, but that is the point. In being specific and vivid they needed to be current. The occasion is the Second Sunday of Lent, Year B: the Genesis 17 version of God's covenant with Abraham, Paul's understanding of that passage in Romans 4, and "Get behind me, Satan" following Peter's confession and the first "passion prediction" in Mark 8. The Holy Spirit wanted to create some space for the listeners to ask some of their own questions, and the preacher used the expression/question, "What were they thinking?" to try and do so.

> Do you ever watch a movie or television show and ask yourself, "What were they thinking?" Who said, "Let's cast Jennifer Lopez opposite Ben Affleck as mob enforcers who have to kill a special needs kid, and they fall in love, except she's gay, and . . . "? Maybe the same people who said, "Let's make a television show about a drug-addicted Episcopal priest whose father is a philandering bishop. We'll give him a nymphomaniac narc-dealing daughter, an alcoholic wife, and a gay son. Then we'll have Jesus look like he came out of a five year old's pop-up Bible story book." You watch *Gigli* or *The Book of Daniel* and you think, "What were they thinking?" It's not just mass media, of course. Who can forget New Coke, the Edsel, or polyester suits? And it is not just funny, not by a long shot. Most of the time we hear what our politicians have in store for us—or in the case of New Orleans, Iraq, health care, and, well, don't get me started—what they don't have in store for us. And we wonder, "What are they thinking?" The same goes for suicide bombers, Muslims who kill Muslims over Danish cartoons, sexually abusive priests, criminally negligent parents, and on and on. What were they thinking? It is also my first, second, and third reaction to the Scripture lessons for today. What were the authors of Genesis, Romans, and the Gospel of Mark thinking?

The only way this introduction is an improvement on the generic introduction to mystery in the first example is if the preacher addresses the spirit of discouragement and distress at current events created by the introduction. This preacher tried, but, and this is a challenge not just for introduction but sermon trajectories as a whole, he may have dug a hole deeper than he was able to climb out of.

Do's and Don'ts for conclusions and introductions

David Buttrick admitted that he wrote *Homiletic: Moves and Structures* with a tone of authority much greater than he felt. The same is true of this book, and in particular of those pages, like the ones to follow, that are explicitly or implicitly replete with, "this is right, that is wrong." So the reader is encouraged to take the following cautions and encouragements as just that. They are not rules.

1. Opening prayers and closing "Amen." It is best not to develop the habit of prefacing the sermon with a spoken prayer like "Let the words of my mouth and the meditations of our hearts be acceptable in your sight, O Lord, our strength and our redeemer" and not to end the sermon, ever, with an "Amen." There are liturgical reasons—nothing should come between the reading of and the proclamation of the Gospel, and because the sermon is not a prayer why do you end it with a prayer formula? There are also practical reasons. Nothing done all the time is heard after a while, so who exactly is the prayer for? If it is for the preacher, it may best be kept to herself. If there are Sundays when the preacher is especially anxious about the sermon, and wants to share that anxiety with the listeners, then a prayer may be appropriate. But the same prayer, especially phrased in a way that requires the preacher to rewrite scripture? No. As for the "Amen," it is both liturgically inappropriate, and kind of needy—like the preacher is encouraging the listener to say aloud something for which they should not need prompting. If they want to say "Amen" that is up to them. You, dear preacher, should leave it alone.

2. Saving enough time to prepare an effective conclusion and introduction. Good intros and endings do not pop magically into a preacher's head in a moment's notice, at least not on a regular basis. They have to be crafted like the rest of the sermon. So the preacher cannot spend all the time available on Scripture study and developing moves in answer to the HQ. Just because crafting conclusions and introductions is last in the process does not mean that no time is budgeted for them. How much? Up to twenty-five percent, the same as for exegesis.

3. Knowing when to stop. Preachers get one conclusion per sermon, and almost nothing frustrates a listener more than hearing a sermon arrive at its obvious conclusion only to discover that the preacher does not realize she or he is done. *Everyone* knows it, and it feels like one could measure the disappointment in the church with a "serm-o-meter" it is so palpable. Do not be that preacher, because it is not just annoying, it undercuts everything that came before the disappointment, and the sermon is lost.

4. Never begin your sermon with a complaint or an apology. Everyone does it. "I don't know what I did to offend (fill in the blank) so horribly that I was assigned to preach today. These readings are impossible,

don't you think?" No they don't. Nor do they want to hear about how you wished you had had more time to prepare. "I am sorry that I did not have enough time this week to do these readings justice" equals, "Stop listening to my sermon now." It is always an amazing honor and privilege to proclaim the word of God. Never complain. The time you took to prepare is the time you took to prepare. They will know if it was enough by the quality of the sermon, so you do not need to give them a warning.

5. The first-person singular in intros and conclusions. I have already cautioned about "hoarding" the first-person singular for the times when it is spiritually and theologically necessary, and homiletically the most effective.[4] Double that caution for introductions and conclusions. The use of "I" in the intro is almost always just a lazy habit. "I went to the movies yesterday and saw . . . ." The preacher is in trouble already by admitting the sermon was crafted in the last twelve to twenty-four hours in the vain hope to show she or he was culturally current; more to the point, who cares? If one wants to say something about a movie character, plot development, etc., just go there. Would one start a sermon with "I decided not to put butter on my popcorn this time. How many of you like butter on your popcorn?" It's more or less the same thing. Get to the point, and most of the time the point is not the preacher. Ending the sermon in the first-person singular should be limited to announcing your resignation. No, wait, save that for the announcements after passing the peace. There is almost no reason to end the sermon talking about oneself. The sermon wants them to be focused on their own lives and faith in response to the sermon, not the preacher's struggle or triumph or *meh*.

Sermon

A sermon for Passion Sunday, Year B (Mark 14:1–15:47), that is almost all intro and ending.

We have just heard a long, sad story with a familiar, tragic ending. Marcus Borg and Dominic Crossan argue that the liturgical recovery of Passion Sunday is necessary because so few of us will return to worship this week

4. Brosend, *The Preaching of Jesus*.

on Maundy Thursday or Good Friday, so if we don't read the Passion gospel now we skip too easily from Hosanna to Alleluia.[5] Point taken.

What shall we make of this story, on this day, calling us to sharp reflection at the beginning of Holy Week? Every time I read it something different catches my thought, but one verse, again and again, year after year, will not leave me alone. Mark 14:50, "And all deserted him and fled."

In the RSV of my upbringing and education the verse reads, "And all forsook him and fled." As Mark tells the story this abandonment is startling, striking. The disciples, led by impetuous Peter, pledge at supper to stand and die with Jesus. Their "stand" consists of one swipe at a servant's ear, then away into the night. We do not know where they go save Peter and a handful of women, who follow, he to courtyard and they to cross. While the Cyrenian may carry the cross for a time, in the most profound way imaginable, Jesus walks the Via Dolorosa and dies on Golgotha abandoned and alone.

I think most of us know ourselves well enough to realize we would do much the same. The truth is, we do it now, every day. Jesus comes, proclaiming the gospel of God (Mark 1:15), and we flee, flee to our private, personal faith, turning our backs on others, and on the community it takes to build and sustain the kingdom of God.

Jesus comes, curing "many who were sick with various diseases, and cast(ing) out many demons" (Mark 1:34), and we flee, flee from the messiness and sadness of illness and suffering, assuring ourselves that our health care system is second to none, give or take the forty-five million fellow citizens without insurance, and a focus on prescription solutions that overlook the prevention that might keep us from illness in the first place.

Jesus comes, and "taking the five loaves and the two fish, he looked up to heaven, and blessed and broke the loaves, and gave them to his disciples to set before the people; and he divided the two fish among them all. And all ate and were filled" (Mark 6:41–42). We flee, safe in the knowledge that we will "always have the poor, and can show kindness to them whenever (we) wish" (Mark 14:7), confident that one day we will in fact wish to help the poor.

Jesus comes, teaching "as one having authority" (Mark 1:22), teaching us to love the Lord "with heart and soul and mind and strength" and "our neighbors as ourselves" (Mark 12:30–31) and we flee, flee to silly questions

5. Borg and Crossan, *The Last Week.*

about the identity of our neighbors, and to the sad truth that we do not even know our neighbors' names.

Our abandonment takes many forms—denial, ignorance, willfulness, fear, dependency, selfishness. Like the young man in the linen tunic, when we run away, we run away naked. It may be dark, so no one notices. But we know. God knows.

We flee, to the intensely personal, protected, and pious. Jesus' execution was public, brutal, and political. All of our well-intended, if ultimately barbaric and futile, theories and theologies of the atonement stumble on this: Jesus did not die for our sins. To say "Jesus died for our sins" sounds like he passed away in his sleep at a ripe old age and remembered us in his will. Jesus did not die, he was killed, by an efficient, violent, occupying power and its local collaborators. We read in a favorite Collect at Morning Prayer that Jesus "stretched out his arms of love on the hard wood of the cross that everyone might come within the reach of (his) saving embrace,"[6] and in Eucharistic Prayer A that "He stretched out his arms upon the cross, and offered himself, in obedience to your will, a perfect sacrifice for the whole world."[7]

Beautiful words. Historical and biblical nonsense. Jesus' arms were stretched out on the cross by Roman soldiers, who held his hands and feet in place while spikes were driven into his ankles and wrists. Jesus did not die for us. Jesus lived for us, fully, faithfully, passionately. And we killed him for it.

Is abandonment inevitable? Is that what it means to take up our own cross—that we leave Jesus to go to his cross alone? That is the question for this Holy Week. It is a personal question, and a question for this and every church. What would it look like for you and me to decide, this week, not to run with the disciples but follow with the women, with Mary Magdalene, Mary, "the mother of James the younger and Joses"—which is Markan code for Our Lady?

Certainly it means not to run from the story but to "read, mark, learn, and inwardly digest" the story, to borrow from another Collect. Set aside time this week to read the first fifteen chapters of the Gospel of Mark. It will take about an hour. Slow down when you come again to chapter 14. Walk with Jesus.

6. *Book of Common Prayer*, 101.

7. Ibid., 362.

Recalling the story is important. Living faithfully in response to the story is discipleship. It is a very political story, with very political implications. Christian faith, rightly understood and practiced, is a way of life in community, not a personal, private set of opinions. Following the women to the cross is feeding the hungry, ministering to the sick, remembering the lonely, encouraging the distressed, and telling the story, your story, of faith, with all its stumbles, all its hopes.

In the chapel of the Cathedral College of Preachers on the close of the National Cathedral in Washington, DC, a chapel now sadly shuttered for a season, is a crucifix unlike any I have ever seen. Jesus, on the cross, does not have his arms "stretched out." His arms enfold someone, someone small, unremarkable, unrecognizable. If you look closely, you will see who he holds on the cross. It is you. It is me.

Chapter Six

Special Occasions

Preaching done as part of the Eucharistic liturgy is always a special occasion. But from time to time one also preaches on occasions that define liturgy and sermon in distinctive ways, and this chapter will consider four such occasions: baptism, marriage, burial, and feast day. On these days the last phrase of the homiletical question—What does the Holy Spirit want the people of God to hear *on this occasion?*—moves to the forefront of the preacher's preparation in ways it does not on a typical Sunday in the middle of ordinary time.

These four occasions (baptism, marriage, burial, and feast day) are distinct theoretically in that they are intensely and explicitly theological in ways that the "Forty-Eleventh Sunday after Pentecost" is likely not. Because the preacher knows these occasions are coming it is possible, indeed essential, to have prayed and studied and thought one's way through theologies of baptism, marriage, death, and resurrection. Twenty-four hours before preaching at the burial of a childhood accident victim is not the time to begin thinking about theodicy and the suffering of innocents. This will be discussed more fully in the next chapter.

Perhaps the most distinctive thing about these occasions from a practical perspective is the dramatic change in the makeup of the congregation, especially for baptism, marriage, burial, and the major feasts of Christmas (Eve) and Easter. While circumstances vary and must be taken into account with each sermon, the preacher can expect to have many listeners who come from a different communion and many other listeners who come from no church affiliation at all. They are there because of the occasion, and often because someone dragged them along, kicking and screaming.

These listeners may be referred to as the "uninterested, unconvinced, and unimpressed," and more than a few are all three. But they are there, must be accounted for, and some of their questions asked along with those the preacher imagines from listeners with whom she or he is familiar. A few guidelines will be considered as these four occasions are explored.

A note of caution by way of a reminder: the homiletical question is still the starting point for preparation, even, for example, in approaching a homily for burial. One is not going to give a eulogy, but a homily, so do not start by asking "What do I want to say about Sally's grandmother?" Nor does one start reading the collected works of St. Swythn to find nuggets to open the sermon on his feast day. The preacher still asks the HQ, does the exegesis, and prepares the moves.

Baptism

Theory

One of the many positive features of liturgical renewal has been the movement away from private baptism. This varies somewhat from communion to communion and church to church, and there are always exceptions, but the regular inclusion of baptism in the Sunday liturgy is not only historically justified, it is homiletically helpful. First, because the preacher is able to draw on the whole of the liturgy in developing his or her theology of baptism in the sermon, and second, when baptisms are regularly scheduled on the days "preferred" by the liturgical year—Easter Vigil, All Saints' Day, First Sunday after Epiphany, etc.—the preacher is able to predictably develop that theology of baptism over the course of the year. You do have a theology of baptism, right?

Pet peeve: preachers who regularly refer to "our baptismal covenant" when there is no baptism taking place. Pet peeve two: preachers who do not refer to baptism when one is about to take place. When that is the same preacher, this teacher is mightily peeved. This does not mean the sermon must always be "about" baptism when one is to take place, nor that the baptismal covenant should never be mentioned absent a baptism; it means the preacher ought to pay attention to the occasion. Is one move too much to ask?

Think of the uncle or the friend of the parents who is in attendance out of familial obligation or friendship, but has not been in church since these parents were married and has not seen a baptism since the last time he watched *The Godfather*. He has no sense of having been baptized himself, and wonders what all the fuss is about even while he bemoans missing the pre-game shows and thinks with dread of the luncheon to follow. He is owed an explanation, and it should be offered in a way that reminds the gathered faithful of the theology of baptism. You do have a theology of baptism, right?

When asking the homiletical question one keeps these listeners, and the families and friends of the baptized, front and center in prayers and preparations. The biblical texts will cover the gamut, and there is no guarantee that baptism will in any way figure into the texts, and if they do it may be so overwhelming (the baptism of Jesus) that there seems little space left for the twins and their big sister who are squirming in the front pew. The preacher has to find, or create, that space.

As a sacrament baptism is a metaphorical treasure trove. It is both particular to Christian faith and order and universal to most world religions. This is why the preacher is able to develop a theology of baptism over the course of a series of baptisms. Baptism does not mean one thing, it means many things: cleansing and purification, forgiveness and healing, passing through the sea in exodus, dying and rising, obedience to the example of Christ, incorporation into the community of the saints. To employ all the available metaphors and meanings into one homily will only guarantee that most of them, and the homily, will be forgotten. The preacher still has to focus.

Practice

Most every time a bishop preaches at a Sunday Eucharist it is part of the annual visitation to the parish, and confirmation will follow, sometimes with baptism. Which means that every time the bishop who is a good preacher prepares the homily confirmation figures into the answer to the HQ. But it does not mean that the bishop always preaches *about* confirmation. The same is true of baptism, and the difference is both important and liberating. How the preacher approaches and prepares for the sermon on a Sunday with baptisms is, as always, through answering the homiletical question. And while baptism will follow, what precedes the homily are the readings, and the preacher cannot ignore them any more than the preacher can ignore the baptism.

The Book of Common Prayer recommends baptism at the Easter Vigil, Pentecost, All Saints', and the First Sunday after Epiphany. Immediately one can see, without looking at a single text, how homilies at baptism on these occasions will (should!) differ significantly. Historically the Great Vigil of Easter was *the* occasion for baptism, after an extended novitiate, and the cluster of symbols and metaphors around "dying and rising" push to the fore. At Pentecost it is the birth of the church and the baptism of the Holy Spirit, at All Saints' it is incorporation into the mystical body of Christ and the communion of all the saints, and on First Epiphany it is following the example of Christ into a baptism for the forgiveness of sins, "adoption" as Christ's own through baptism and the connection to Judaism and all religions which practice ritual lustration. How could one possibly have a "baptism sermon" to be trotted out as needed, "insert names here"?

Which means the preacher lets the liturgy do some of the work. Easter Vigil, Pentecost, and All Saints' are high holy days, with powerful readings, prayers, litanies, and associations. The sermon latches on to that with all its might. Even on a "low" Sunday with baptism there is significant liturgical "oomph," a less familiar form that sends even seasoned regular worshipers scurrying to prayer book or program, with extra processions and prayers, water and oil, adorable infants and recalcitrant toddlers. The preacher uses all of it.

And, of course, there are the biblical texts. Allowed to handpick a text for preaching a baptism one could do no better than the epistle for All Saints' Day, Year A, 1 John 3:1–3.

> See what love the Father has given us, that we should be called children of God; and that is what we are. The reason the world does not know us is that it did not know him. Beloved, we are God's children now; what we will be has not yet been revealed. What we do know is this: when he is revealed, we will be like him, for we will see him as he is. And all who have this hope in him purify themselves, just as he is pure.

It is a sermon sketch, if slightly out of order: we are God's children, "purified" in baptism, and though "what we will be has yet to be revealed" we imagine marvelous things.

Equally suggestive are the lessons for the First Sunday after Epiphany, Year B. The readings begin with the beginning—"In the beginning God created the heaven and the earth. And the earth was without form, and void; and darkness was upon the face of the deep. And the Spirit of God moved upon the face of the waters" (Gen 1:1–2, KJV)—then tell of disciples who knew only the baptism of John and had not heard of the Holy Spirit (Acts 19:1–7), and Mark's account of the "baptism of our Lord," which pays more attention to John the Baptist than to Jesus (Mark 1:4–11). Here the preacher may want to emphasize traditions and connections that relate baptism to creation, redemption, and Spirit ("brooding over the face of the deep").

At the Easter Vigil the faithful read Romans 6, "Therefore we have been buried with him by baptism into death, so that, just as Christ was raised from the dead by the glory of the Father, so we too might walk in newness of life" (Rom 6:4) but usually not until *after* the baptism. This does not mean that it cannot be mentioned. However, the readings at the vigil are recounting the history of salvation in which water—at creation, the flood, the exodus—is prominent. How powerful to craft a sermon in which those to be baptized are entering into this history! The biblical possibilities are as richly suggestive as they are seemingly endless.

Texts and baptism are central to the occasion, but there are also people. Those to be baptized and their families and sponsors, and those who witness and will pray, "We receive you into the household of God!"[1] or something similar in other traditions. Not everyone in the church can be mentioned by name, although usually the candidates for baptism will be. But everyone in the church can be included in the homily. "Remember your baptism, and be glad!" And perhaps something like this, somewhere along the way in the homily: "We are going to make solemn vows to do everything in our power to support these persons in their life in Christ. What do you think the statute of limitations on those vows is? This week? A couple of years? To tell you the truth we should not be surprised if twenty years from now one of these children of God march down the center aisle and says 'Hey, a little help here!' We should rejoice."

A Sermon on the occasion of baptism, All Saints' Day, Year A (Revelation 7:9–17; Psalm 34:1–10,22; 1 John 3:1–3; Matthew 5:1–12)

Heaven has been waiting for this day for all eternity. All Saints' Day, this year, for all eternity. You can tell by the smell, the sweet savory mix of incense, beeswax, flowers, and diapers, the smell of baptism. The book of

---

1. *Book of Common Prayer*, 308.

Revelation tells us that a crowd that cannot be numbered is gathered around the throne of God, worshiping the Risen One. There are new faces in the crowd this year, some of them very dear to us, the farewells said in this church still echoing in our lives. After they finish another round of Handel's "Hallelujah Chorus" and the glorious concluding "Amen!" the saints will join us, from their distant shore, as we gather around the baptismal font. This is a great day, a glorious day. A day of memories and a day of hope, a day of vows and a day of blessings.

A priest in a neighboring tradition is fond of waving the aspergillum on Sundays with baptism during the procession into the church, and the procession to the font. He likes to use a lot of water, and shout with each wave of the arm, "Remember your baptism, and be glad!" "Sometimes," he said, "you have to really soak them. But usually it only takes a few drops on the face to wake them up, so they can remember."

Do you remember your baptism? Not many of us can honestly say that we do, in the sense of closing our eyes and recalling how it felt to be held in the priest's arm and the shock of the water on our forehead. Not all of us are "cradle" Episcopalians, however, so we may be able to. But that is not the point, not what my friend has in mind when he shouts, "Remember your baptism, and be glad!" It is a much deeper remembering, recalling who we are as a child of God, beloved in Christ, for whom astonishing promises have been made. And everyone who ever made a promise on our behalf is present with us on this All Saints' Day, in this communion of worship and hope.

Why, after all, do we make promises and vows? Surely it is enough to intend. Why does saying it out loud, and tossing in a little water, make a difference? I can think of more reasons than you will want to sit still for, so let's settle for this—while we have all sometimes failed to keep our promises, no one ever keeps a promise they did not make. Until good intentions are given voice that is what they remain, good intentions—and you know what road they pave.

The epistle reading makes two promises, one for today, and one forever. "Beloved, we are God's children now; what we will be has yet to be revealed. What we do know is this: when he is revealed, we will be like him, for we will see him as he is." In this the epistle is not unlike the Beatitudes, which begin in the present tense but stretch into promises for a future yet to be revealed. What comes between today and forever? Our own promises, and the unfolding of those promises over our lifetimes.

The promises that will soon be made at the font are ridiculous, impossible, and maybe even a little pretentious. They are, I think, overwhelming. Which is why we make them together. Make them alone and you will fail. Make them together, blessed by the Holy Spirit, and all heaven is going to break loose.

It happened recently at a church not so far from here. The parish imagined what it would look like to make folk feel as welcome in the nave at worship on Sunday morning as they tried to make them feel welcome in the basement. Calling it the "undercroft" did not help when you went downstairs for the twelve-step meeting, the food pantry, the counseling center, and the once-a-week overnight shelter for the homeless, and upstairs to worship, Christian formation, choir practice, and the parish offices. They started by having Bible study and prayer downstairs, by being present at the dinner and breakfast for the homeless, by repeating the invitation to "come upstairs"—and here is the hard part—being ready to welcome someone when they did.

Heaven, we know, has also exploded into the homes and lives of the families we will join around the font. It is a crazy, chaotic, sleep-deprived heaven, but if it is not a taste of "on earth as it is in heaven" I do not know what is. Jessica and Randall, Anna and Thomas, Elizabeth and Marie, you need to know two things. The promises you are about to make are at least as impossible as the vows you made at your marriage. Trust me, I was there. You cannot do these things for Sarah, Timothy and William, and Molly. But we intend to hold you to these promises, every word of them. Not fair? Hey, you are parents, so you might as well get used to "It's not fair" sooner rather than later. But here's the deal: we are going to make promises too, and we demand that you hold us accountable to our promises as well. That is how this works, and without our doing this together, that is how it collapses. The minute you feel that we are not here for you call us on it. And the minute we feel you are uncomfortable asking us for help, we will do everything we can to change it.

This communion, the communion of all the saints, is the fellowship into which Molly, William and Timothy, and Sarah are being baptized. It is older than the ritual we share and as new as the promises on our lips and in our hearts, vows recreated in our speaking. It is as deep as the love of God, filled with possibilities yet to be revealed to us. It is good to be here. Heaven has been waiting.

Marriage

Theory

Unless they are born romantics, a few years into ordination many clergy begin to dread the celebration of a marriage, and say in unguarded moments that they would trade ten funerals for one wedding any day. It is a terrible thing to say, and a worse thing to feel; but it is a common feeling. Why might it be true? It is a long litany, from mothers-of-the-bride to wedding planners, photographers to inebriated groomsmen or bridesmaids, the fact that with a rehearsal, dinner, and wedding reception it can "ruin" the weekend, unless the clergyperson runs the risk of offending by skipping the dinner and reception. There are exceptions, of course, relatives and longtime parishioners, the couple who found each other after terrible losses, etc. But sadly, over time exceptions do prove the rule. Were one to pinpoint why many clergy feel the way they do about the Celebration and Blessing of a Marriage, and why the contrast with funerals is so great, it is this—while clergy are needed to say "I now pronounce you" they otherwise feel irrelevant to the entire event. And to some extent based on what is going on in the hearts and minds of those gathered for the occasion, the preacher is irrelevant. The disconnect is present in the language itself. The priest and pastor is present to bless and consecrate a marriage; pretty much everyone else has come for a wedding ceremony.

This is a dreary way to begin a section on preaching at a marriage, so perhaps some good news is in order. For while they will often forget to include the celebrant in the photos, if one does the job well they will not soon forget the homily. During those moments the preacher is anything but irrelevant, and if she or he remembers to ask and answer the HQ, keeping in mind the couple and the occasion but not jettisoning the lessons or the questions of the listeners, a good beginning is made. Also keep in mind what makes preaching at a marriage distinctive, because in very important ways the only audience for the homily is the couple being married. *When we preach a marriage we are preaching to the couple.* Others are welcome to listen, but they are overhearing what is said to the couple. The sermon is not *to* those in the pews, it is for and to the couple.

Dr. Craddock introduced this idea in his Yale Beecher Lectures published as *Overhearing the Gospel*.[2] It remains essential reading for those who would be good preachers. Born of a long conversation with the work

2. Craddock, *Overhearing the Gospel*.

of Søren Kierkegaard, the lectures argued that indirect communication was more effective than what we might now term "in your face" communication, and that people "overhear" with much greater attention than they hear directly. So fear not, preacher, even though the sermon is directed to the couple, others will be listening. However, if the couple are only bit of stagecraft and the sermon is aimed over their heads to those in the nave who undoubtedly have some work to do on their own marriages, no one profits or is delighted.

In the best of all worlds the preacher knows the couple well, if only from the canonically mandated pre-marriage counseling sessions. In the worst case they have attended some classes led by someone else and the preacher does not have a clue. So the preacher is going to have to meet with them or give the opportunity to preach to someone else. Let's assume the best case. Preparation, then, is a combining of what is known about this couple and their hopes for their marriage, what the church believes about marriage (you do have a theology of marriage, right?), and what the readings chosen for the day suggest. Answering the HQ therefore happens with an extra layer or two. Fortunately in many traditions, including Anglicanism, the biblical options are circumscribed, and exegesis is soon less onerous. Until some couple picks Tobit 8:5–8.

They are more likely to pick 1 Corinthians 13 and the Beatitudes, which gives the preacher more than enough to work with. The homiletical question is now phrased, "What does the Holy Spirit want this couple to hear from these texts on the occasion of their marriage?" And one of the elements of sermon preparation difficult for many—focus—is immediately ready to hand.

The homily at the celebration of a marriage is brief, usually five and no more than seven minutes long. A marriage is an *occasion*, so the focus is not on the readings, and certainly not on exegesis. If a preacher even thinks about offering an expository sermon on Ephesians 5 to share how masterfully he or she teased out the implications of the *haustafel* in the pseudo-Pauline epistles in a seminary term paper, chant "TMI, TMI" until the feeling goes away. There is time for one move, two at most, and this does not leave time to explore Tobit and explain the origins and canonical status of the Old Testament Apocrypha.

The homily is brief, and so must be tightly focused. Usually what the Holy Spirit wants the couple to hear is that their marriage is gift and blessing, that the gathered faithful rejoice with them and pray for them, and that the Spirit's guidance and help is always available to them. The preacher wants to find a way to personalize this message for this couple, then stop. Discourses on the "assault on marriage," examples from the preacher's years of experience working with other couples, interesting tidbits from cultural anthropologists about how marriage has changed over the centuries, and just about everything else a preacher is tempted to toss in the homiletical stew has no place.

Practice

The key to crafting a marriage homily that is for the couple and will be overheard by the congregation is to craft a homily for the couple, period. In the best of all liturgical worlds the couple sits for the homily in the chancel, facing the nave, while the preacher stands to the side, back to the nave. If great grandmama has trouble hearing that is okay, as long as the homily was really for the couple. Once "overhearing" becomes a device, and the turn of the preacher's back an affect, almost everything is lost, and the homily is really for no one.

The preacher has more time to prepare a marriage homily than a burial homily, and should take advantage of that fact. And, as with the burial homily, the range of texts is delimited in liturgical traditions, so two things should be true: it is possible to lay and draw on a strong exegetical foundation over time, and it is possible to build on that foundation by restudying texts, and reading new literature about them. Saying to oneself "I've preached a dozen marriage homilies on these texts so I do not need to explore them for this one" avoids the homiletical question and cheats the couple. While the preacher may know for months or longer in advance that she or he will be preaching this particular marriage, however, does not change the fact that on the week of the marriage it is often not the only homily the preacher is preparing. So this caution: do not default preparation time to the Sunday homily when the fact is there will likely be more people attending the marriage than the Sunday Eucharist, and there will certainly be more un- and barely churched people.

There is one other practical way in which preparation for the marriage homily is similar to preparation for the burial homily—the preacher has the privilege of conversations that allow the actual questions, not the imagined or reconstructed questions that the primary listeners bring to this occasion, to shape the homily itself. Which is a roundabout way of saying that good preachers use their time with the couple to prepare the couple for marriage and the preacher for the homily. Pre-marriage counseling at its best is catechesis.

Most preachers find over time that the biblical texts for marriage are not as homiletically suggestive as the texts for baptism or burial. The Old Testament speaks far more often of adultery/idolatry than of marriage, and some of the best known Old Testament marriages (Hosea, anyone), are a little problematic. The only "weddings" in the Gospels are more about the party than the liturgy, and do not usually end well. Just ask the foolish virgins in Matthew 25 and the guy who showed up without a tux in Matthew 22. Moreover, building elaborate, while quite biblical, analogies between marriage and the church is probably going to both bore and confuse.

Which takes the preacher back to square one, the homiletical question, and to the realization that one is preparing for an occasion that is much more liturgical than biblical. The prayers, the hymns, the procession, the gestures, the rings, and the vows are also texts, and should be treated as such. If you find yourself exegeting the words of the "Blessing of the Marriage,"[3] go with it.

As a rule, the preacher does not talk about his or her own marriage at all, and if so only in passing, as in the example below. To begin, "I would like to share what I have learned about marriage in my own life" is an offense punishable by a Zechariah-like nine months of silence. Nor does one begin, "You two are either brave or foolish, maybe both, because fewer and fewer couples are getting married these days and half of those who do will wind up divorced." The preacher does not try to be clever, impress, or amuse, call attention to nervousness or past expressions of anxiety or hesitation, etc. Remembering that the sermon is for two people, and preparing and preaching accordingly, eliminates many, if not most, potential problems.

This violates the principle that one speaks differently to an audience depending on its size, but nothing is never and nothing is always in preaching. Do not worry about what anyone else in the church hears, thinks, or responds to this homily; give everything you have to the two being married.

Sermon for a marriage (1 Corinthians 13:1–13)

Look at you two! Glowing! Everybody is here, a glorious party awaits, where I am told your fathers have promised to dance. You have been at showers

3. *Book of Common Prayer*, 430.

and receptions, opening scores of cards and gifts and will depart the dead of this early winter to Aruba. Folks are lining up to carry your bags.

And so, obviously, we stop right in the middle of everything to worship. What, really, could make more sense than that? To give thanks to your Creator, to pray in the name of the One who perfectly embodied love, and to seek divine blessing on your life together, pray God your long and wondrous life together.

The only part of this that does not make sense is me talking. What do I know? Yes, I married spectacularly well, thank you Jesus, and we have been blessed with amazing children, but what does my marriage have to do with yours? Nothing. And this is really the thing—just about everything anyone else thinks they know about marriage because they are married is irrelevant. Every marriage is unique. So be polite, but don't listen to them. I told you that the first time we met in my study. You will find your own way. There is one person whose advice I do want you to take seriously, which is weird because someone tried as hard as possible to keep him from coming up today. You remember when we were choosing the readings for your liturgy and Heather said, "I like the 'love chapter' a lot" and I sighed? Thomas caught me and wanted to know why I moaned. Okay, I didn't sigh, I moaned, and audibly. I have been thinking about my dumb answer ever since, and about my resistance to applying the words of 1 Corinthians 13 to your marriage. Now I have a good explanation—I was wrong.

You told me that one of the reasons you love each other is that you do not feel like you have to explain yourself to each other, that you can just be who you are that day and know that it is okay. Paul wrote that "love bears all things, believes all things, hopes all things, endures all things. Love never ends." You also said that there was a rough patch or two in what we could quaintly call your "courtship." Paul wrote, "Love is patient; love is kind. Love does not insist on its own way." The apostle was not writing about marriage, but everything he wrote is about marriage. If we cannot live as Christians in our marriage, how in heaven do we expect to do it anywhere else? So Heather, you were right; thank you.

In other traditions and other ceremonies couples often write their own vows as a way of trying to capture the uniqueness of their love. That's cool but that's not us. The vows you share today are older than English. What is unique about your marriage is how you fulfill those vows. You, Thomas and Heather, have been fortunate to be around some folks who have done quite the job of living their own vows. Obviously Heather's grandparents, whose sixtieth anniversary is coming soon, your grandfather having robbed the cradle big time. But this church is filled with those examples, some of them "standing up" with you who boast whole entire months of married life. I am not contradicting myself. I know I told you to ignore what they say about marriage, and do ignore what they say. But do not ignore what they do, how they live out their vows.

A lot of words will get tossed around today and you will not remember 98 percent of them, including mine. But I want you to remember the words of the reading you chose from 1 Corinthians.

> Love is patient; love is kind; love is not envious or boastful or arrogant or rude. It does not insist on its own way; it is not irritable or resentful; it does not rejoice in wrongdoing, but rejoices in the truth. Love bears all things, believes all things, hopes all things, endures all things. Love never ends.

At the reception tonight they will remove the tiny top layer of your wedding cake and freeze it so that you can share the delicious taste of year-old cake on your first anniversary. To help you remember the words of the apostle I asked them to bake a little laminated card into that top layer. I am not kidding. Ask Heather's mom. It won't do much to help the taste of the cake—freezer burn is freezer burn. But remembering those words will flavor your marriage forever.

Burial of the Dead

Theory

"I do not know what to say. We are so sorry for your loss." The purpose of the homily in the Burial Office is simple and profound: the preacher is to speak for the church, to the family and friends of the deceased. Simple. The preacher finds the words that others cannot, and speaks for them. Profound.

The preacher speaks the words the church cannot find to the family and friends of the deceased. Each element is important. Just as the marriage homily is for the couple and not the congregation, so the burial homily is for the family and not for the gathered friends. They overhear, but they overhear differently than those at a marriage because they are listening to hear if the preacher is saying what they wish they knew how to say, if their love and loss and compassion and grief is being adequately expressed. And the preacher speaks to the family. Not, "the preacher proclaims the good news of eternal salvation." Very little, maybe nothing, will sound like proclamation; the burial homily is intimate. Good news is shared, but at a whisper, with a lump in the throat.

Biblical texts are the great friends of the burial homilist. The texts put into words what for all one's practice and skill one still cannot: hope. The psalms are more important here than at any other time in preaching; and as crazy as Paul may drive one in other places, to preach without Romans 8:31–39, 1 Thessalonians 4:13–18, or 1 Corinthians 15:51–58 is to preach empty-handed, with nothing to give. One does not exegete the texts from the pulpit; they speak or they do not based only on the power of the words. If the preacher feels the need to say, "Now Paul was probably writing the Letter to the Romans from prison, so his words really take on a new meaning," he has lost all sense of the occasion. One does not talk about the dependent nature of sheep; one prays Psalm 23.

Texts without theology are not enough; we cannot share hope we do not have. We can fake it for a while, but if Qoheleth's "all is vanity" is our personal conclusion, it will not last. The work of preparation for the burial homily likely began in childhood, for some more poignantly and powerfully than for others. But all ask "Why do people die?" and "What happens to people after they die?" early in life, and unless one is satisfied one keeps asking the question. Good preachers are never satisfied. This work undergirds preaching but is not a part of preparation for any given burial homily. There is not time. And as will be discussed in the next chapter, this work is hard work. One reads Karl Rahner and Paul Ricoeur, not Mitch Albom (with all due respect).

Every death is hard because every life is precious, but some burial homilies are easier to prepare—if hell to deliver—because the preacher knows the deceased, the family, and their faith. Then the preacher can affirm with joy, and tears, that our song at the grave is indeed "Alleluia, alleluia."

Other times one is not able to share a personal affirmation, and when this is not possible one must not do so. Rule: when we cannot affirm the faith of the deceased we affirm the faith of the church. The preacher does not posthumously award a faith no one was aware of in life so that he or she can talk about "seeing them again in heaven." Repeat after me: *When we cannot affirm the faith of the deceased, we affirm the faith of the church.*

Preachers will also encounter times when the only thing anyone can affirm is that the deceased was about as rotten a human being as anyone has ever known. This is the time, and this comment is not in the least facetious, when it is wise to remember that *The Book of Common Prayer* says "Here there *may* be a homily."[4]

Finally, and as far from facetious as one can imagine, are times that are unspeakably hard, and when in fact the preacher has no better words than anyone else, because there simply are no words. A child has died, or a classroom full of children. A car full of joyous teenagers has been crashed into by sleepy trucker, or a mother has been taken from her children by disease. Pick your poison, because if you preach for more than a little while it will be your turn. And you will pray for words that will not come. If ever there is not a time for pat answers, empty assurances, and saying something you do not believe with all your heart, it is this homily. If what you can say with all your heart is "This is the hardest day of my life as a preacher" then that is exactly what you should say, and explain why. Name the pain, and do not imagine a Never Never Land where everything will be better. This terrible, tragic, life-shattering loss is not "a part of God's plan." This is evil. It will be redeemed but now is not the time, nor should you imagine that it will be redeemed by your homily. God did not "want them more than we did" or any other absurd and heretical sugar-coating a preacher might imagine. Look the family in the eye and say, "I do not know what to say. We are so sorry for your loss."

Practice

"Some funerals are hard," the preacher said. "But this is not one of them." He went on to contrast the death of a teen with cancer, or a young soldier on the battlefield, with the death of the ninety-year-old whose corpse rested in the casket before the congregation. What he was saying was, "Heh, why are you grieving? It was time." Just what the family needed to hear from the church.

The list of things one must not say in a burial homily is long, and the only way to avoid them is to have enough things that should be said. There is usually not much time to prepare; even when a death is long-expected rarely does a preacher prepare a homily in advance like *The New York Times* prepares obituaries. So the homiletical question must be asked, and the direct input of the family and friends must be sought in the time between death and burial or memorial service. Because while everyone may think

4. *Book of Common Prayer*, 495.

they will know how they will feel when the long-dreaded death finally comes, they do not know until it does, and the "occasion" moves from the abstract to the very, very real.

The preacher's preparation is therefore both long term and immediate. One reads, studies, reflects and prays toward a theology of death and resurrection from at least the first studies in seminary to retirement. Then the preacher meets with the family, selects texts, hears their stories of the deceased, and stays up half the night preparing the homily. There is no substitute for either form of preparation. The night before you preach is not the time to discern your theology, and because the loved ones of the deceased cannot know how they feel, what their questions are, etc. until they have been separated by death, all the "pre-decease planning" (is that what the funeral industry calls it?) in the world is of no help.

It cannot be stressed too greatly: sitting with the family sometime after the "Ministration at the Time of Death"[5] is indispensable, no matter how well the preacher may know the family. If you do not know them at all, it is a necessity. There are details to review and decisions about texts, hymns, readers, and so on to be made. And there is a pulse to be taken. The preacher cannot speak for the church into a generic vacuum of "grief" but speaks to this loss, this grief. So it must be gauged. The preacher is also looking for something, something that will be used to organize the words of the homily in a way that allows the family to hear it. For lack of a better homiletical term this is called a "hook." It is not the hook with which we are trying to grab something, but the hook we hope to "hang" the homily on. The hook needs to come from the deceased and the family. It needs to be a part of their relationship, a part of their collective memory. And it needs to ring true (to mix metaphors) to everyone in attendance, so the family says, "That's him all right" and the church says "I could not have said it better myself."

Hooks come in many forms. It may be a defining personality trait, "She was such a kidder," or a habit or hobby, "He would rather fish than eat" or "We put knitting needles and yarn in the casket because we have never seen her without them. Is that okay?" It could be a love of music, art, or theater, a passion for Jane Eyre or Cormac McCarthy, a devotion to *La Virgin de Guadalupe* or the local Habitat for Humanity affiliate. It may be "noble in the sight of all" or a personal commitment or relationship. The deceased loved what she or he loved, spent their life the way they did, and

5. *Book of Common Prayer*, 462-67.

the hook is not a moral judgment; it is a homiletical tool. What it has to be is true. Early in ministry a preacher was asked to officiate at the burial of the cousin of a parishioner. After talking with the family nothing emerged, not sports, the arts, the community, certainly not the church, to help the preacher understand the man. Finally someone said, "Well, he did like his beer." It was a start.

How the preacher deploys the hook she or he uses is by suggestion, allusion, analogy, and tangent, not by saying, "The best way to understand so-and-so is through x." This approach is a primary example of Dr. Craddock's teaching that good preachers leave something for the listener to do, in this case "hang" their own experiences with the deceased on the homiletical hook the preacher has placed before them. If he told corny jokes one need not recite a list of them; the one they told you about tossing a package of frozen fish filets to his grandson at the grocery store and saying, "Catch! I told you I'd take you fishing" will do. Letting the listeners fill in the blanks from their own memory is infinitely more valuable than running the gamut.

Using this hook allows the preacher to make the homily personal without devolving into a eulogy. It is still a homily, with the personal aspects developed as a move within the overall homily without seeming like the preacher is reading an obituary. The task is not to summarize and praise the life of the deceased, but to speak for the church in ways that affirm faith, share love, and embrace grief. To borrow an analogy from painting, preachers use the broad brush strokes of Impressionism, not the detail of the Renaissance. The listeners see it or they don't.

Like the homily at a marriage, the burial homily is brief, five to seven minutes. The liturgy does most of the work, and one does not need to repeat it, or attempt to preempt it. Scripture is often effectively woven into the homily, and when that happens it must be recited by heart, not read, if it is to have much impact. Only then can it speak from heart to heart. Since the preacher has not died, there is no point in talking about what you know about death. Since everyone has experienced loss and grief, and is experiencing it now, the first person singular is mostly unnecessary. Speak for the church, not of the church.

Funeral Homily

> For I am convinced that neither death, nor life, nor angels,
> nor rulers, nor things present, nor things to come, nor
> powers, nor height, nor depth, nor anything else in all cre-
> ation, will be able to separate us from the love of God in
> Christ Jesus our Lord (Rom 8:39).

The Apostle Paul made more outrageous claims in his seven letters than the rest of us make in a lifetime, but this one may take the prize—nothing can separate us from the love of God in Christ Jesus our Lord. Nothing? Then why are our hearts broken today, why have our words failed so completely when we greet Tom, Elizabeth and Andrew, Charles and Mary, and Robert? Why can we only hug each other and cry? Nothing, Paul? You obviously did not know Alexandra. We do, and right now God is feeling pretty far off.

Do you remember when you were first smitten by Alexandra? For Mary I suppose it was a kick in the womb, for Charles the first time he heard her heartbeat, and for Robert when they brought his baby sister home from the hospital. She was a child of this parish and many of you go back almost that far—to her baptism and confirmation, her service as aco-lyte and youth group terror, then leader. You missed her when she left for college, delighted when she was home for a holiday and came to St. Mark's to worship with Mary and Charles, intrigued when on one trip she arrived with a handsome, obviously smitten, young man named Tom in tow. A few years later there was a marriage celebration at least the music director will never forget, when most of her college choir came to quadruple the number of choristers. Because they too had been smitten by Alexandra.

God, Scripture tells us, was smitten first. "Before I formed you in the womb I knew you" God said to a prophet of old (Jer 1:4), and was not that what Alexandra was among us, a prophet, that is, one who spoke God's truth, called us to account, and imagined how things could be different, better, just about every day? Even as she was dying with cancer. Yes, God was as smitten with Alexandra as we all are, which makes this so hard, so very, very hard, and Paul's words so ridiculous. Nothing, Paul? This broken heart, this Gibraltar-sized lump in the throat sure feels like something.

I do not know what to tell you to do because I do not know what to do with my own grief. I was smitten in my first meeting with the rector search committee, and that was on the telephone. So let me tell you what I feel. I feel that we have much, much more to do to honor and remember

Alexandra, and to support Tom, Liz, and Andy, her parents and brother, and all who love her, which means all of us. We have talked about what tangible form that might take in our parish and community. For today and tomorrow it takes the form of keeping her name on our lips, her family in our prayers, and being annoying in including them in our lives. They will tell us when to stop bringing food or inviting them over; and by the way, Andy is "allergic" to brussel sprouts and broccoli, just like his mother.

Many of you have said that Alexandra was the "most alive person" you ever knew. She still is. As Paul wrote elsewhere,

> Behold, I tell you a mystery. We shall not all sleep, but we shall all be changed, in a moment, in the twinkling of an eye, at the last trumpet. For the trumpet will sound, and the dead will be raised imperishable, and we shall be changed (1 Cor 15:51–52).

It took much more than a moment for Alexandra to be changed. She fought this cancer for seven damn years, not the seven months she was told at diagnosis. For you, for all of us. She was smitten with cancer, but she smote it right back. As she herself often said, cancer is a bastard, and you never let the bastards win. They didn't. Alexandra died on her terms, in her bed, with her family.

Paul said nothing could separate us from the love of God in Christ Jesus. So why do we feel so distant and alone? Because Paul forgot to mention something—grief. Is there anything holier than grief? Than tears and sobs and fists of anger, shaken at God in grief? Is there anything more faithful, more hopeful, more loving, than grief?

Dear family of our beloved Alexandra, we grieve with you, we grieve for you, and we hold on to this, that God grieves with us, grieves with us the grief of faith, hope, and love, the faith, hope and love that defined Alexandra to her last breath, describes her even now, and forever.

Feast Days

Theory

Feast Days are often a challenge for preachers, especially lectionary preachers accustomed to devoting a large proportion of sermon preparation time to biblical exegesis. Many are more comfortable taking apart the intricacies of the twentieth chapter of the Fourth Gospel than they are exploring a theology of resurrection, and their Easter sermons show it. The problem is that what these days are about is not what happened in the biblical text, but what it means, and good preaching on these days is decidedly theological, not exegetical. It is all too easy to spend thirty minutes on Easter morning, Year B, discussing Mark's elaborate ways of telling us how very, very early in the morning it is when the visit to the tomb takes place, comparing the empty tomb in Mark's "shorter ending" with the resurrection appearances in the other gospels, and not say anything about the meaning of the resurrection of Jesus. Adult forum and the Easter homily have become terribly confused.

Feast days come in two kinds, major and minor, not "red letter days" and other solemn occasions but "big, bold, underlined, italicized red letter days" and all the rest. Other than the obvious—Christmas (Eve), Ash Wednesday, Maundy Thursday, Good Friday, Easter, Pentecost, Trinity Sunday, All Saints' Day—how to distinguish major from minor is decidedly a matter of the community in which one preaches. In some communities Marian feasts, from Annunciation and Visitation to Presentation, are paramount, in other communities not a peep. If it is feast day of the saint for whom your parish is named it matters a lot, if it is not, the "Confession of St. Peter" may slip by unnoticed. Moreover, some days, while decidedly secular in origin, like the Fourth of July, bump into the liturgy, and sermons, in unavoidable ways. The preacher must sort it all out.

By and large most feast days invite decidedly theological sermons. What does that mean? In general it means one should consider preaching on the themes and doctrines suggested by the biblical texts and the occasion. Trinity Sunday casts around for any text that hints at God in three persons, and so lands on "the Great Commission" (Matt 28:16–20) in Year A. To decide to preach theologically is to focus on "in the name of the Father, the Son, and the Holy Spirit." But the preacher may also feel that what the Holy Spirit wants is for her or him to focus on "Go." One sermon focuses on Trinity Sunday, the other on the mission of the church. How does the preacher decide? The preacher doesn't decide. The preacher asks the HQ and lets the Holy Spirit decide. Jesus is born and baptized every year. Is the sermon "about" the incarnation or baptism, or about shepherds in first-century Palestine or ritual lustrations in world religions? Feast days invite the former in particular ways.

This invitation asks many preachers, not just the author, to preach outside of our comfort zones. Telling listeners what is the consensus of biblical scholarship on a given passage is less risky that telling them what that means, and the meaning of what that means for the life of faith, *their* lives of faith. What we know about ancient Mediterranean understandings of eternal life is not exactly the same as discussing the life after death of those listening to our homily. Usually one talks about taking homiletical risks in the context of so-called "prophetic preaching" on money, war, human sexuality, and other ethical topics. It turns out that theological preaching may be even riskier.

Practice

So, preacher, what is your theology of creation, atonement, incarnation, Holy Trinity, virgin birth, resurrection, ascension, forgiveness, and assorted other terms that often begin with capital letters? Not sure? What better way to work on it than preaching on it?

Preachers often avoid or postpone working out their own theologies in relation to Scripture by regularly preaching some version of an expository sermon, "walking through the texts" to make sure the Greek grammar is clear when what the listeners want to know is why Paul had such an issue with "law." The suggestion of this chapter is for the preacher from time to time, especially on feast days, to elect to do otherwise, and plan on preparing specifically theological sermons unless the answer to the HQ suggests otherwise, because such sermons generally require more preparation than exegetically centered sermons. Why? Lack of practice. Preachers do not need to study more, they need to reflect more, and they need more time to craft illustrative material that will turn theology into "lived religion."

Pick a major feast day, any major feast day. In some traditions such days are still sometimes referred to as a "day of obligation." The preacher owes it to Jesus, and to the listeners, to show up. Take the Feast of the Transfiguration, which may not be major to everyone but is certainly in red letters. The exegetical key is that what is depicted is the glory of Christ in his second coming, not Bultmann's "misplaced resurrection appearance." So the theological question is why depict this glory pre-passion, and why the church does so twice a year, on Last Epiphany and August 6? No other narrative in the Gospels is similarly used. It must be important. What is the theological importance of the Transfiguration? This is very different than asking, "What does the Transfiguration mean for us today?" and then talking about all the changes in our lives. This is about Jesus, the Christ, the Son of the Blessed.

The Transfiguration affirms the baptismal voice, and validates the voice of the One to whom we are commanded, "Listen to him!" Not just in the promise of the resurrection, but in the promise of the final fulfillment in glory. Somewhere between *Elmer Gantry* and *Left Behind* we lost sight of the fact that the promise of the End is a promise of hope and fulfillment, substituting neo-apocalyptic for biblical assurance. The Transfiguration, interpreted eschatologically, is a reminder that Christ's return will be as triumphant and gracious as it will be unmistakable.[6]

Now the preacher is ready to ask, "What does this understanding of the theological implications of the Transfiguration mean for our life of faith?" as opposed to "How can we be changed like Jesus was changed?" We can't be. That is not in any way what the Transfiguration is about, and to start by confusing *metamorphōsis* with "change" (Gk. *allassō*) is to be theologically doomed. How does the saying go? Ask better questions.

Not every feast day is "major," and while observance of *every* feast day is limited to rare environments like mine in Sewanee ("one part Oxford, one part Mayberry, one part Brigadoon" said retired dean William Stafford in my hiring interview), favorites happen everywhere. And unless given a chance one will never know what favorites might be waiting to be discovered. This preacher was forever captivated by the "wise and cheerful boldness" of twelfth-century Anglican bishop Hugh of Lincoln after being asked to preach on his feast day. St. Francis, St. Teresa of Avila, Thomas Merton: pay attention, preacher. One approaches them not by abandoning the HQ and looking for something, anything, by or about them but reading what is available, when that is possible, and allowing that to figure into ones answer, as in the example below for the day when the Episcopal Church commemorates John Henry Hobart.

Finally, one other suggestion from Dr. Fred Craddock—the annual sermon. In the Baptist tradition in which I was raised this would be "Homecoming Sunday." In my beloved Anglican tradition this would be the patronal feast day. The texts are fixed, and according to Dr. Craddock, so is the text of the sermon. The patronal feast day is a day when the parish remembers who it is, what it stands for, and what it is called to be in the world. That does not really change from year to year. So Dr. Craddock suggests that the preacher offer the exact same homily every year, word for word, reminding the gathered faithful who they are, where they came from,

---

6. Brosend, "The Feast of the Transfiguration," 161.

what they stand for, and what they are called to be in the world. Amazing. Does the structure become staid, and the illustrative material boring? Quite the opposite. It is more like Ezra reading the Torah at the reinauguration of the Feast of Booths, the faithful waiting to hear the familiar words. Unless God has changed the parish's call, it can be a powerful reminder.

Sermons

A sermon for the Feast commemorating John Henry Hobart, John 17:11b–21

The Fourth Gospel devotes more than four chapters to the "farewell discourse" of Jesus. Scholars of John's rhetoric have shown us that the most characteristic feature of these 134 verses is repetition, perhaps to the point that chapters 14 and 16 are different "performances" of the same discourse. Why bring this up? Because what is repeated again and again in the "discourse" is equally important to the "farewell prayer" from which we just heard. Jesus is keeping faith with what he has emphasized throughout the Fourth Gospel. The same themes—his abiding relationship to the Father, the promise of such "abiding" to his disciples, the possibility of fulfillment in joy tempered by the dangers of the world—are all here. This focus, keeping all that he received, keeping faith, guarding and watching and praying; Jesus in John's gospel knew how to keep it real.

Focus. In this political season they call it staying "on message," and it is not as easy as it seems. You could make a pretty good case that the devil's primary twenty-first–century tactic is distraction. "Squirrel!" Taking this day as an occasion to read some of the sermons of Bishop Hobart, I was reminded just how hard it is to stay focused. God knows it seems to bedevil most preachers.

We do not make much of Hobart in Province IV, perhaps as our way of staying loyal to William Porcher DuBose. Like DuBose, Hobart was instrumental in the founding of a seminary, THE General Theological Seminary they like to remind us. He was also instrumental in turning Trinity Wall Street into one of the largest landowners in Manhattan, and as bishop in supporting the founding of scores of parishes in New York state. Scores of churches. Fr. King might even concede that Hobart had an influence on the Tractarians, at least as to form. Who knew the stream flowed in that direction?

But I teach preaching, so what I confess admiration for is the focus and discipline of his published sermons. In an age when preachers had barely cleared their throats in the first hour, Bishop Hobart brought it home in twenty minutes. And while he had not read Dr. Craddock, so we need to give him a pass on the whole inductive turn, his sermons were a model of rhetorical clarity. When he said he was going to offer three reasons why something was true, or should be done, or might change your life, he told you three and then sat down. Praise God. The man kept his promises.

In the farewell discourse and prayer Jesus reminds the listener/reader that he has also made good his vow. He kept faith with his Father, and with his disciples. It is for this hour that I have come.

This is the point in the sermon when the preacher challenges the members of the congregation to keep the vows they themselves have made, and an assortment of vows tossed about as examples. Wedding vows come quickly to mind, and that favorite of Episcopal preachers, especially seminarians, the baptismal covenant. You know I am not going there, as exalted and important as they surely are.

I am more interested in the vows you have made to yourself, the promises that expressed your greatest desires and deepest hopes, vows you have not dared to speak aloud. The vows we remember in final summations and taking stock of our lives. Farewell discourses and prayers, from Jacob in Genesis and Moses in Deuteronomy to Steve Job's amazing Stanford graduation speech and Carnegie Mellon professor Randy Pausch's "last lecture," are a rhetorical staple of most traditions. They do many things, not least, they remind us of the vows we have made to ourselves in our best moments. What are those vows? When it is your turn to offer a farewell discourse, a final prayer, what will be worth taking time to mention? What vow do you imagine will stand the test of time that is your own life? Bishop Hobart, in a sermon on James 4 about the dangers of a "deathbed confession," encourages us to write that speech now, and instead of spending our lives wondering what we will say with our last breath, spend our lives living what we know we would vow if we were blessed with a "deathbed confession." Jesus put it more or less the same in the "parable" of the watchful servant.

The trouble with keeping our vows is that doing so often gets in the way of keeping faith with our vows. One view would argue that the church has fought its greatest battles between those who come to believe that keeping faith with their vows required them to "break" the vows themselves. Vows of obedience readily come to mind, but even vows of chastity—when men or women religious are called to marriage—and vows of poverty, when a community raises funds to preserve facilities or provide for new ministries. The church may until its last breath struggle with the difference between keeping the faith and keeping vows.

If the history is complicated the personal can be a full catastrophe, and I will not bore you with my own details. The vows we made a while ago did not anticipate the challenges we face today. More significantly, they did not anticipate the opportunities we face today.

The simplest solution is to make no vows. It is a culturally ascendant solution, but you gave up on that a long time ago or you would not be in Sewanee. Wendell Berry is our teacher here. The things we vow to keep will change, and will change us even as we lose them in our keeping.

> Some had derided him
> As unadventurous,
> For he would not give up
>
> What he had vowed to keep.
> But what he had vowed to keep
> His keeping changed
>
> And, changing, led him far
> Beyond what they or he
> Foresaw, and made him strange.
>
> What he had vowed to keep
> He lost, of course, and yet
> Kept in his heart. The things
>
> He vowed to keep, the things
> He had in keeping changed,
> The things lost in his keeping,
>
> That he kept in his heart.
> These were his pilgrimage,
> Were his adventure, near
>
> And far, at home, and in
> The world beyond this world.
>
> —WENDELL BERRY, *Given*

A sermon for the Great Vigil of Easter
(American Cathedral in Paris, 2016)

We have just heard some amazing, amazing words, words to remember, words to live by. I hardly know where to start, and I know I don't know where to end.

"I'll make me a world!" And God said, "That's good!" (Gen 1/J. W. Johnson).

"Let my people go!" ("Go Down, Moses").

"Prophesy to the bones, prophesy to the breath. . . . I will put my spirit within you" (Ezek 37:6).

"Do you put your whole trust in (God's) grace and love?" "I do." "Will you continue to . . . persevere . . . proclaim . . . seek . . . serve . . . strive?" "I will, with God's help." "Let us welcome the newly baptized." (Baptismal liturgy).

"So that we too might walk in the newness of life" (Rom 6).

"Why do you look for the living among the dead? He is not here, but has risen" (Luke 24).

Wow! But there is one other word we need to hear clearly tonight, from God.

NO!

On Maundy Thursday and Good Friday we sat and watched as the powers of this world did their worst to the very best that God had to offer, God's own, beloved Son. As the preacher said, "Jesus did not die for us. Jesus lived for us. And we killed him for it."

Tonight, tomorrow, and for all the days thereafter we live in and into God's response. Jesus did not die for us. Jesus lived for us. And we killed him for it.

> And on the third day, GOD SAID NO!
> God said NO to the power of Empire.
> God said NO to the power of hell.
> God said NO to the power of death.
> NO!

And in that divine no rings out the eternal YES of Easter. God's yes. Not power but peace. Not hell but heaven. Not death but life, eternal life, life in fullness and abundance. We call it "resurrection." Tonight God's no to the powers of death, destruction, and damnation also proclaim God's yes to life, hope, and salvation.

During these three holy days we have been considering the basic Christian practices of the Triduum. Thursday the practice was service. Friday the practice was forgiveness. Tonight's practice is the practice of our lifetimes—resurrection. We owe this wisdom to the Kentucky author, environmentalist, and poet, Wendell Berry. In "The Mad Farmer's Liberation Front" we read in part:

> So, friends, every day do something
> that won't compute. Love the Lord.
> Love the world. Work for nothing.
> Take all that you have and be poor.
> Love someone who does not deserve it. .
> Ask the questions that have no answers.
> Invest in the millennium. Plant sequoias.
> Laugh.
> Laughter is immeasurable. Be joyful
> though you have considered all the facts.
> Practice resurrection.

Eight years ago President Barack Obama called his campaign "manifesto," if one may use that word, "The Audacity of Hope." Remember eight years ago? Even with the former governor of Alaska in the mix that was a civil campaign by current US standards.

Hope is always audacious. Hope is one of the ways we practice resurrection. Hope is what we just practiced at the baptismal font. You said some things a few minutes ago I pray Caspar Louis, Lawrence Brooks, and their families, will come back and remind you of. You promised, after all. We promised without thinking about it. Now I want you to think about it, because vowing to "do all in your power to support these persons in their life in Christ" may involve diapers. Someone may need a babysitter, a tutor, a shoulder to lean on, an ear to bend. You promised, and that, dear people of God, is to promise to practice resurrection.

We have been talking about practices. Others call them habits, ways of being, the shape of living. Thursday night I mentioned that when a musician is preparing a piece for performance we call that "practicing." But she is making music, just as surely as she is during the performance. When we practice resurrection we are making real the joy of Easter, the miracle of faith, hope, and love discovered in, of all places, an empty tomb. Why do we seek the living among the dead? We have had enough of death and destruction. We were made for resurrection, for life, for hope.

The *world*, to use the Gospel of John's preferred term, practices manipulation, exploitation, self-seeking, and death. We have had enough of that. We don't want more, we want different. That is why we are here. There are those who exploit loss, terror, disease, borders, un- and underemployment, and all the rest in order to manipulate people and foster fear. Sadly, right now in the US and elsewhere these manipulators are running for public office, offices low and high. We must join God in saying "No!"

Practicing resurrection means rejecting exploitation, scapegoating, fear-mongering, and demonization as dialogue, because those of us who practice resurrection are fearless, welcoming, and hopeful.

Practice resurrection, because the power of love is greater than power of hate, because the power of hope is greater than the power of fear, because the power of life is greater than the power of death. The tomb is empty. The children have been baptized and we have made promises.

Some will doubt. Practice resurrection.

Some are cynical, sardonic, urbane. Practice resurrection.

Some will threaten, shout, and shoot. Practice resurrection.

Wendell Berry must be heard:

> So, friends, every day do something
> that won't compute. Love the Lord.
> Love the world. Work for nothing.
> Take all that you have and be poor.
> Love someone who does not deserve it.
> Ask the questions that have no answers.
> Invest in the millennium. Plant sequoias.
> Laugh.
> Laughter is immeasurable. Be joyful
> though you have considered all the facts.
> Practice resurrection.

Chapter Seven

Style, Delivery, Practice, and Evaluation

> For there are three qualities that are considered—volume, harmony, rhythm. Those who use these properly nearly always carry off the prizes in dramatic contests, and as at the present day actors have greater influence on the stage than the poets, it is the same in political contests, owing to the corruptness of our form of government. But no treatise has yet been composed on delivery, since the matter of style itself only lately came into notice; and it is rightly considered to be vulgar. But since the whole business of Rhetoric is to influence opinion, we must pay attention to it. (Aristotle, *Rhetoric* III.I.4–5)

Preaching is an oral medium. You are reading a book, perhaps on your e-reader, but still in print, silently, to yourself. That is not what this book is about, so the disconnect is obvious. From the first chapter this book has tried to keep those listening to our sermons before us throughout the discussion of the sermon preparation process, emphasizing that the homiletical question is never about what the preacher wants to say, but what the Holy Spirit wants the people to hear. Yet until now focus has not been on the mechanics of "how" that hearing happens. That is the focus of this chapter, and also on finding ways to allow the hearers to respond directly to their own encounter with preaching in order to help the preacher do better the next time. Finally, attention will be given to the habits and practices that shape the lives of excellent preachers. The format of this chapter will differ from the seven before, because it is all practice, not much theory.

Style

Preachers often pretend to themselves that they are faceless, selfless, unremarkable sharers of Divine truth. They are not. They have style. It may be self-effacing, dour, or introverted. It could be gregarious, glib, and outgoing. It does not matter. What matters is that the preacher recognizes his or her personal style, and *decides* how that style will be reflected in her or his preaching. Because as weird as this may seem, the decision about the most effective style, and delivery, is part and parcel of the answer to the homiletical question.

The first thing to be said about one's preaching style is that it must be authentic. Do not misunderstand homiletical authenticity, however. Advising a preacher to seek an authentic style is not saying "Just be yourself." Instead it advises that our style of preaching must be congruent with who the preacher is, and grow out of her or his personality as well as faith. One no more has a preaching *persona* (Greek for "face") than one has a pastoral care *persona*, a staff meeting *persona*, or a confirmation class *persona*—even though the way of being present in each of those situations may vary considerably. Preachers must be themselves in the pulpit, but it is the self "amplified."

The second thing to be said about preaching style is that it is a decision that comes from the answer to the homiletical question, so what is being considered is not style but styles. Preachers whose style never changes have opted for a particular understanding of authenticity over effectiveness. The elements of style of concern in this section—position, posture, and manuscript/notes/nothing (voice, movement and gesture will considered in the next section)—do not have a single answer, world without end, amen. Effective preachers adapt their style to the occasion, and do so authentically.

The preacher asks from what position can this homily be preached most effectively: the pulpit or lectern? Behind the altar? The top of the steps leading to the chancel? In the center aisle just in front of the first pew? Moving from one place to another? These are legitimate matters of style. But the answer is not, "Well I really feel more comfortable walking around, so that is what I do." You, dear preacher, want to feel comfortable? That is not style, that is self-indulgence. What position will help your audience better hear what the Holy Spirit wants them to hear in this homily? That is the only legitimate approach.

Architecture and audio frequently answer this question for us. In a high church, gothic-revival nave with a pulpit from here to eternity and one, fixed-position microphone the preacher is using the pulpit, period. In more contemporary spaces, or less formal liturgies, the preacher is able to consider other options. The occasion also defines the answer—if the preacher is a guest she tries as best she can to do what the host does, and the listeners expect. A Maundy Thursday homily focused on Holy Communion could well be shared by the table; one centered on the foot-washing to follow the homily might be shared beside basin, pitcher, and towel. If sight lines and audio quality allow, a homily on the occasion of baptism could be given from beside the font. These are decisions, not preferences.

Posture, or perhaps more fully, demeanor, is also a matter of style. How preachers stand, how they hold themselves, the expression(s) on their faces, are part of their style and a crucial aspect of communication. Some things are obvious. Stand up straight and confident. Do not put your hands anywhere you did not intend them to be. Do not lean on anything, ever. Smile enough to relax the face and jaw but not so much that you seem deranged. Give the appearance of someone who really, really wants to be right where you are. And this, although some might prefer it discussed under delivery: bring all the energy you and the Holy Spirit can muster. Energy. Enthusiasm? Sort of. Passion. That's it. Passion. Energetic passion. Not maniacal homiletical style, but deep passion that leads to preaching with energy. It may be calm and quiet in delivery, but the energy and passion are still riveting.

The final topic in this section is the most contested: does the preacher use a manuscript, notes, or nothing, so-called "extemporaneous preaching," which, pray God, it should be anything but. Note first that this is a question of style, not of preparation or delivery. In general, and especially for new preachers, a complete manuscript should be prepared for every homily. Whether the preacher uses the manuscript, or makes notes from it that then may or may not be sufficiently rehearsed to allow preaching without notes, is the question. Good preachers prepare oral scripts or written manuscripts; they just do not always use them in the act of preaching.

Every word in this book assumes the preacher prepares a manuscript. But that does not mean the book assumes everyone should be a "manuscript preacher." Far from it. The hope, although this is the goal not the starting point, is that the preacher is able to do all three with equal effectiveness— delivering (not reading) a manuscript, preaching from notes, or presenting the sermon without either, which is what the author prefers and does when there is adequate time for preparation. This cannot be stressed enough.

Preaching without notes is not a shortcut to anything; doing it well takes much more preparation and practice time than delivering a manuscript. But one still prepares the full manuscript if at all possible. Why bother? Because the words will be clearer, more colorful, and less repetitive, and the arrangement of the moves and transitions between them more effective. Phrasing that is crafted and revised is almost always more memorable than phrasing chosen at the spur of the moment. The purported values of preaching without notes are just as available when one has prepared a manuscript and has the mastery not to employ it. This is also just as true from the pulpit as it is when "stalking the aisles." People sit in the last row for a reason; the preacher who gets too close may give them no choice but to walk out the door!

Can style be both authentic and affected? Yes, but only from time to time. As suggested in the quote from Aristotle at the head of the chapter, preachers are at a certain level actors, and more will be said about this below. The liturgy is the drama of salvation, and the preacher has a part to play in that drama. When the role is one believed in deeply, when the role of preacher in the liturgical drama is fully inhabited, preaching thrives. When the preacher does not believe in the role, perhaps for that Sunday because of something that happened that week, or because the biblical texts have been a particular struggle, or vacation starts tomorrow, then to be honest it is a good thing to choose to be "in character" as the preacher. When one does not believe in the role because one's time with these children of God is drawing to a close, or a sabbatical, not a vacation, is needed, one cannot hide behind the role, and must seek out the help that is needed. Authenticity demands it.

Delivery

Having decided in answering the HQ questions of style and demeanor for this sermon, where to stand and whether to use manuscript, notes, or nothing, and being fully committed to preaching with passion and energy, be it a quiet, meditative liturgy like that for Ash Wednesday or a raucous celebration of Pentecost, other questions remain. How will the homily be delivered? Is it wise to use something—props, film clips, song snippets—to heighten interest, and if so how should these "somethings" be deployed? What about gestures and movement, in or out of the pulpit? Here are three "rules" to begin with: (1) look up; (2) slow down; (3) speak out.

Few things are as off-putting to an audience as someone who is bent over his or her manuscript and reading as if they are seeing it for the first time, suggesting that either they have not practiced or they did not write the manuscript. Deadly. Just as awful is the manuscript reader who has made notations throughout to "look up," which leads to periodic head bobbing without eye contact, and sometimes the preacher accidently saying "look up" in the middle of explaining a tidbit of biblical or theological minutiae. Good preachers give the appearance of never breaking eye contact even when they are in fact reading a manuscript, occasionally looking down when need be but doing so with their eyes, not their heads. How is this possible? Proper positioning of the manuscript and plenty of practice. Many pulpits allow the position of the manuscript to be adjusted, others can be jerry-rigged, and in still other places the preacher's stance can be adapted to create the ideal sight line. This does not happen on Sunday morning. If the preacher is new to a parish she or he plans to be in for a while it is well worth whatever expense is required to make needed changes. The other element is practice, knowing the manuscript and moves so well it is not necessary to read each word, even each line. More on the guidelines for this below.

Slow down. About once every one hundred seminarians the homiletics professor may have to urge the student to pick up the pace because the sermon is lagging. The other ninety-and-nine are told to slow down because no one can listen as fast as she or he can talk. Three factors are at play here. First, based on changes in the delivery pace of national news broadcasters, we are all apparently listening more slowly than we used to, likely a reflection of how visual our lives have become, with purely aural media declining in popularity. The second factor is that the larger the audience, the more slowly they listen. "Conversation" is a popular metaphor for preaching, and to the extent it highlights the dialogical nature of preaching, and the intimacy one brings to the proclamation of the kingdom of God, well and good. But if it leads the preacher to think she or he does not need to modulate the pace for the size of the room and the number of people listening to the homily, it may encourage a pace that is in reality much too quick.

Finally comes regional differences; i.e., accents. It is simply easier to process the words of someone who "talks like us." If the preacher's accent reflects a regional difference, she or he will need to slow down even more, especially in the introduction. If our accent reflects a national difference, that is, we are not speaking in our native language, we may need to slow down still more.

Here is the simple guideline: 80 to 120 words per minute is as slow and as fast as we should preach. If the custom and expectation is a twelve-minute homily then your manuscript may be 1,000 to 1,500 words long. You cannot prepare 2,000 words and decide to just preach real fast that Sunday. After a while each preacher knows how long it takes to deliver a given number of words, and prepares accordingly. Become that preacher.

No matter how fast or slow, loud or soft, solemn or excited, speak out. In the day of over-the-ear wireless microphones this may seem silly, but it is not. The microphone, of whatever style, must be positioned so that the preacher may speak out, and so can modulate his or her voice through its full range. If the preacher has to whisper because the microphone is too close (watch out for the explosive "p"!) or the sound system is turned up too high, make adjustments. On Saturday. Articulation and enunciation is also a part of speaking out. And often a part of slowing down. It may seem like a vacuous compliment, but having someone say, "I really liked your sermon; I could hear every word" is anything but. It is an absolute necessity.

Having learned how to look up, slow down, and speak out, the preacher is able to think about how to use voice, movement, and gesture to strengthen delivery. The key idea is emotion; the most helpful analogy is the theater. The expression is "a full range of emotions." Joy, sorrow, anger, anticipation, eagerness, and so on. This range of emotions is often expressed in sermons, given how widespread the emotions one finds in biblical texts. Most have no difficulty expressing a range of emotions in conversation. So why not use them in preaching? Students will be talking excitedly in the hallway, then come in and preach with all the affective range of a sloth. The use of emotions in preaching has to be done with authenticity, and so with gestures. If one needs to write a note to make a gesture, "pound the pulpit now," then for heaven's sake do not bother. It happens or it does not happen.

The analogy for how to employ emotion, motion, and gesture is the theater, not television or film. Not the amplified, animated, projected-on-the-screen touring productions in huge auditoriums or arenas, but smaller theaters, Broadway to off-off-Broadway, a handful to a few hundred in the audience, no microphones, no close-ups, nothing between the actors and the audience but the orchestra pit, if that. Yet every word is heard, every gesture and expression seen, in the last row of the top balcony. Even the whispers. How do they do that? They project. They express emotion from the inside. They do not move without a purpose or make gestures incongruent with their words. Yes, they are acting, but we forget that with the good ones, don't we?

A word about props: no. Same with film clips, skits, and singing from the pulpit. If, and this is a big, big if, the answer to the homiletical question inescapably suggests you sing the introduction to your sermon, or use a clip from your favorite movie, or have the ushers bring a huge ladder into the nave so you can perch on it and preach about Zaccheus, then the answer is NO! Remember, of course, that nothing is never and nothing is always in preaching. Don't sing!

I know you are going to ignore this, so a few suggestions: (1) On the occasions when you plan to use a prop, a film clip, or sing somewhere in your sermon you have to practice those too. Especially if it involves technology. Frozen screens, clips that suddenly take too long to buffer, or skip or pause, and songs you sing off key are worse than nothing, scuttling your sermon and undercutting the liturgy. If you are going to do this you need to be as smooth as the late Steve Jobs introducing the iPhone (and yes, there was chaos behind the scenes). If the film clip does not pop up exactly when it is supposed to, that is your fault, not that of the teenager pressing "play" off to the side. (2) Take a hard look at the unintended consequences of your stagecraft—if the listeners refer to your sermon as "the one with the fork" because you stood in the pulpit waving a fork and said something about "eat dessert first" you are in trouble. (3) If the Holy Spirit moves you to sing a verse or two every other sermon, and your name is not Renèe Fleming or Beyónce, ask yourself about the homiletical objective of your performance.

On the plus side are two things largely absent in contemporary preaching well worth commendation: silence and memorization. Silence is largely, sadly, missing from our worship. And it is rarely used in preaching because preachers, insecure as they are, do not want the listeners to think they have forgotten their place and do not know what to say next. We need to get over ourselves. Even five seconds of silence after a powerful or poignant move will greatly magnify the impact. The same is also true of memorized material, usually poetic, often biblical. Experienced preachers rightly caution against the overuse of quoted material. It can confuse the listener unless one uses some awful formulation like "end of quote." For the most part this is material so familiar everyone knows it did not come from the preacher, from the Psalms to Shakespeare. But if the preacher declaims it, from memory, with the full range of appropriate emotions, it can have an impact far beyond what simply reading the words would have.

Preparation

Do you practice what you preach, or do you just preach it and hope for the best? As one gains experience, or becomes familiar with a new space, the need to unlock the doors of the church on Saturday, turn on the sound system, and climb into the pulpit decreases. But the need to practice the sermon, out loud, does not.

There is a huge assumption here, the assumption that the preacher has prepared far enough in advance that he or she has something meaningful to practice on Saturday afternoon. That is not always the case, but if preachers are honest it is true more often than not. (It is noticed at preaching conferences that preachers tend to "dumb themselves down," talking as if they rarely prepare adequately, or before Saturday at midnight. Pray God this is false modesty.) So instead imagine a best-case scenario.

The HQ was given a preliminary answer a couple of weeks ago, the biblical texts and pastoral life simmering together, then times of exegesis, sketching moves, confirming the answer to the HQ and four or five moves beginning to take shape a few days before the sermon will be preached. On Thursday or Friday morning the sketch and the moves are drafted, arranged, and the conclusion and introduction written. The manuscript preacher is done, except for practice. The note and "naked" preachers have to fashion a short outline from the manuscript, which then becomes the basis for practice. These notes are not extensive, a few words to describe the move and a reminder or two about its direction; there may be room for a quotation which will need to be memorized.

Now it is practice time, which begins the same way no matter the style but ends differently. The preacher first reads the manuscript aloud, has a cup of coffee, and does it again. The manuscript preacher will read the manuscript aloud five or six more times in the next twenty-four hours. Note, this is not five or six times silently in the hour before worship. The purpose of the practice of reading the manuscript aloud, with an interval in between, is to become so familiar with the words, page turns, or flow of the iPad that it becomes automatic. Those preaching with or without notes also want to rehearse the manuscript to allow the phrasing and transitions to sink it, but also practice, out loud, in the manner in which she or he will preach on Sunday. Everyone practices, out loud, a number of times and with intervals in between. The one preaching without notes must memorize those notes, but not the words of the manuscript. Some of those words, no matter how spectacularly crafted, will be lost in the preached sermon. That is the price of preaching without notes. There is not, of course, much time to do this in a sermon for the burial office.

The power of effective sermon delivery is a tool far too few preachers utilize, as if the work, and the potential for impact, is over when the manuscript is crafted. If that were true the ushers should just pass out copies after the reading of the Gospel and all wait until everyone is done. This would have the advantage of saving time, because people can read a lot faster than they can listen. Historically we do not do so because preaching is an oral medium whose roots go back to a time when most listeners were illiterate. Rhetorically we do not do so because an effective delivery magnifies the impact of the manuscript. These days the listeners are often better educated than the preacher. But they still listen, incredible as it seems every time we stop to think about it. Their willingness to listen deserves the preacher's best efforts in not only crafting the sermon, but delivering it.

As one grows in experience so may one also grow in the willingness to experiment, not only with different styles, using notes if one almost always uses manuscripts, for example, but with different deliveries. Here the analogy is television or film, where the director asks the actors to reshoot a scene multiple times, but do something different, emotionally, in each take. Experienced preachers give themselves the freedom to experiment with emotional range, within their own limits of authenticity. In the voice of a gifted preacher like the Presiding Bishop of the Episcopal Church, the Most Rev. Michael Curry, the divine name has anywhere from one to a half-dozen syllables, from "God" to "Gaaaaawwwwwwddddddd!" depending on what is called for in answer to the HQ. Louder or softer here? Practice it both ways to find out. Do I know this portion of the psalm for the day well enough to proclaim it by heart? Practice and see. Practice. Maybe even revise a little more, and practice again.

Evaluation

One's attitude toward evaluations vary to the extent of one's self-interest. If a website or hold time on a telephone call is annoying us we may volunteer to take the "short survey at the completion of this call." If asked to complete an evaluation after a conference we dash something off on our way out the door. If required to perform a formal evaluation of the parish staff, knowing that they are doing the same, everyone takes time and takes care. If asked if they would like to have their sermons evaluated far too many preachers duck and cover, remembering how awful it felt in seminary when the professor asked for comments after a practice sermon and everyone looked down at the floor.

Time to grow up. The only way preachers can improve is by evaluation and coaching, asking how this particular sermon "worked," how it might be more effective and what that means for the next sermon, then evaluating that next sermon. Evaluation is not for the thin-skinned; it is essential for those who want to improve. As much as the seminarian may have dreaded in-class evaluation it is not long before she or he realizes that other than settling for a "nice sermon" from someone while noticing someone else who stormed up the side aisle to avoid all contact, the preacher is responsible for making sermon evaluation happen. There are three ways to do this, apart from asking spouse, partner, or children. They increase in the degree of difficulty.

The first and absolutely essential is self-evaluation. Any preacher who reaches back in the file to see what he or she did three years ago knows that this can be painful. However, three years is too long to wait. Once a month is about right, and the discipline is to watch, or at least listen to, the sermons recently preached. One is looking for tics, repetition, clarity, and logic. One also makes note of the use of illustrative material and where that is clustering (Too many movie references! Too much sports!). Self-evaluation allows for brutal honesty, if the preacher is willing to be honest with him or herself and can remember what the working answer to the HQ was for that sermon. But it does not allow the preacher to gauge in any way the impact of the sermon on the listeners. Truth be told, preachers can dazzle ourselves and perplex listeners at the same time.

The second form of evaluation is parochial, and should happen annually. If there are multiple preachers on staff it should include all of them. This requires more work, and more vulnerability, but the format is not difficult. Two to four sessions are required, depending on how many sermons will be evaluated. Epiphany is a great season for this exercise. A group of six to eight parishioners (no retired clergy, chaplains, etc.), all whom the preachers respect and trust, is required. These should not be six to eight of the preacher's best friends. Trust and respect, not affection, is what matters. The sermons must be videotaped so that attendance on the same Sunday at the same service is not required. A one-page evaluation guide is helpful. While the letter of invitation has explained the purpose you begin by restating your desire to get real feedback on the effectiveness of your preaching. Then you watch a sermon and discuss it. Someone else moderates the discussion, not the preacher. After the first sermon they will say, "Nice sermon." After the second they may blast you. And then the pendulum settles and you are given helpful feedback on sermons three and four. Wait a year and repeat; half the group should also repeat, half the group should be new.

The third, most time-consuming, vulnerable, and valuable form of evaluation is with preaching peers. This group meets once a month or so, often discussing the upcoming lessons, but also has taken the time to watch online one or more of the sermons recently preached by members of the group. Ideally this group is facilitated by a homiletics professor or experienced preacher. In other situations the roles rotate around the group —someone is host, someone leads the discussion of upcoming lectionary texts, and someone facilitates the discussion of a sermon from a recent Sunday. The value of this group, other than collegiality and a head start on sermon preparation, is that the evaluation goes beyond "I liked that, this was helpful, that was confusing" to "what if you tried it this way?" One's colleagues may be in position to make concrete suggestions for improvement in ways our parishioners are not.[1]

Some preachers want more. Preaching "coaches" are sometimes available. Others choose to enroll in a Doctor of Ministry in Preaching program. Both these options cost money and time, and are not for everyone. Evaluation, however, is for everyone, and is the best way to grow as a preacher when formal education for ordination or lay preaching license is complete, and preaching conferences few and far between. Every profession requires evaluation; most require recertification. What is good for the listeners in their fields is good for the preacher as well.

Practice

Self-evaluation and openness to the evaluation of others is a discipline, or what might better be termed a habit or practice. Craig Dykstra, Dorothy Bass, Timothy Sedgwick, and David Ford are among those who have taught us about the importance of Christian practices as a way of ordering,

1. Hiers, "Peer Mentoring for Preachers."

shaping, and enriching the life of faith. There are also a set of practices, including evaluation, that enrich what Barbara Brown Taylor so memorably called "the preaching life."[2]

Prayer. Many good preachers have a prayer life that is in shambles. This is known because they say so in their sermons, cautioning others to do what they say, not what they do. This is hard to believe. What is more likely is that they have compartmentalized their prayer life and not noticed the thousand ways they may be praying every day. What they need is not more time for prayer, longer and better retreats, or a new spiritual director. What they need is awareness and attention, and the realization that they *are* praying, they just aren't moving their lips or closing their eyes. Preparing and preaching a sermon is a profound form of prayer, one that can leave preachers with a void when for a season they are not called on to do so. It is at that moment, with so much extra time to pray, that they experience the inadequacy of their prayer lives. This is not of course a recommendation that preachers stop reading the Daily Office or praying the hours, cease spiritual direction and skip their next few retreats. It is an invitation to preachers to stop beating themselves up for not having the prayer life of a medieval monk, to approach and appreciate their sermon preparation as an offering to God, and to be present, aware, and awake to the movement of the Holy Spirit as they read and reflect, craft and edit, and finally as they step into the pulpit. Breathe in; breathe out.

Study. There are two kinds of preachers, a caricature because obviously there are those who fall in between, but in general there are preachers whose bookshelves groan with the latest additions in theology and biblical studies and history, and those who might as well have left their books in their seminary apartment because they have not cracked an old one or bought a new one since ordination. It is one thing to take a break after three years of intense study. It is another to think that three years of study will sustain one's preaching forever. Good preachers never stop learning, never graduate. They try to "keep up," not in every field, because that is impossible, but in their favorites. And they read not in the hope of finding something for next Sunday in a lectionary commentary, but in the hope of more fully understanding demanding material. They read things they did not have time for in seminary, or the newest book by their favorite professor. Here's the thing about valuable study—it is not done for the sake of tangible homiletical reward, it is done for its own sake, for the love of

2. Taylor, *The Preaching Life.*

the topic and the love of learning. Good preachers "keep up" not because anyone is asking but because their self-understanding includes being the sort of preacher who stays current in the field, even though in this case the "field" is comprised of a half-dozen different disciplines. Time for study is different than time for sermon preparation, although there is obvious overlap, and so remember one piece of advice from chapter two: go deep, not broad. You will learn more from working through one challenging work in an important and favorite discipline than skimming across three or four. Reading Charles Taylor's *A Secular Age* will serve the preacher better than reading a half-dozen popularizers who can say what is happening in various churches today, but not why. Better to (re)read Raymond Brown's *The Death of the Messiah* in Lent than a lectionary commentary for the Sundays of Lent. The former is study that will inform preaching for a decade, the latter is sermon preparation for the next six weeks.

Listening. It has been remarked on a number of occasions how audacious it is that people sit and listen to us preach. It is an honor one should regularly and irregularly return. It is first the difference between politely waiting for your turn to speak and truly hearing what someone else is trying to say. Deep listening. And not "I think I hear you saying . . . ." Much deeper than that. Compassionate listening, hearing where their great-grandmother's voice is echoing in what and how they share with you. That kind of regular listening is one of the great privileges of the pastoral life. Preachers learn the practice of deep, compassionate listening not to benefit the next sermon but to ground all of their preaching in the lives of their listeners. Irregular listening is attending to the conversations of those who will never hear a sermon, the conversations going on all around every preacher, the conversations preachers have but pay no regard to. At the gym and the store and the game, with the cab driver and waitress and dry cleaner. The Episcopal Bishop of Olympia goes to a bar on Monday night where he is only known as "Greg" and talks with folks while watching a game. That is a good practice.

Reading. The author is a middle-class white male living in the mid-South, a seminary professor at a prestigious regional university. Lots of privilege, but without effort a very small world. The antidote is reading, lots of fiction because it is a way to hear the voices of others whose lives are vastly different. The list is so long there is no point in sharing favorites, but this is the shortcut: the Sunday Book Review in *The New York Times*, *The New Yorker* magazine, which publishes poetry and a short story in every issue, plus regular fiction collections, and the annual edition of *Best American Short Stories*, which gathers twenty or so of the best stories from journals and magazines each year (and which is required in preaching classes). Other preachers use movies or film to accomplish similar goals, but because preachers use words, not images, a steady diet of people who use words extraordinarily well (so this includes poetry—there are four in every issue of *The New Yorker*) enhances preaching in other ways. If reading is not your thing, you could try audio books. If you have a good public library, use it, support it, and volunteer for it (a good way to meet people who share some of your values but hang out in a different corner of the kingdom of God).

Schedule/flexibility. Two related practices are essential to excellent preaching: having a schedule and learning how to adapt when your schedule unravels because of life and ministry. If you stop and ask the vestry or governing body in your communion how much time they would like you to spend preparing your sermons, or simply tell them that you need X number of hours per week, plus a study retreat and a meaningful continuing education experience each year it is almost guaranteed they will say, "Great!" They have as much interest in the quality of your preaching as you do, maybe more. If you do not squander this opportunity it will reward you. When you make out your schedule pay attention to your bio-rhythms, your work habits, and how you have experienced the inspiration and intervention of the Holy Spirit. It can be difficult to say in effect, "Okay, God, I need you to meet me on Wednesdays from 2–5 PM, take it or leave it because that is when I am pulling the sermon together." While many good preachers are able to take an entire, uninterrupted day to craft their sermons, it is better to find two blocks of time, a couple of days apart, to plan and sketch the sermon, with a third block of time to craft the manuscript. Lots of good things tend to happen in the "between times." A block for reflection and the preliminary answer to the HQ, a block for exegesis and sketching the moves, with time in between for additional experience and inspiration, and a block for crafting the manuscript. Make sure that one of those blocks is during your most productive time of the day. And then be prepared to watch it all fall apart as the realities of the lives of your parishioners, your family, unexpected emergencies, etc. snatch the time away. This means learning the skill of flexibility, and especially of learning how to use thirty minutes well—one more reason to craft the sermon as a series of moves. Thirty minutes is not enough time to craft a twelve- to fifteen-minute homily, but it is enough time to work on one move. Finally, if you find that everything, every week, seems to push your sermon preparation to the side because everything seems more important or urgent than Sunday's homily, call me. That's a problem.

Pray, study, listen, and read. There is one other thing, not unrelated but still distinct: *have a life.* All work and no play makes for really lousy preaching. Because everything the preacher does, sees, hears, tastes, and touches finds its way into sermons eventually, so everything is part of our sermon preparation. Sort of. One must still find six to eight hours per sermon for intentional preparation and crafting. In between are other aspects of the work of ministry, and time for focused study. And preachers also need to make time for the work of doing nothing, the work of doing whatever one wants, and the work of doing what the others in the family want and need. In other words, have a life. You are going to regularly encourage your listeners to take time for themselves and their families and cherished relationships. That is excellent advice. Take it, preacher.

Sermon for Proper 26, Year A (Micah 3:5–12; 1 Thessalonians 2:9–20; Matthew 23:1–12)

My family says that I am a contrarian. I disagree. Oh. Okay, maybe I am, which could also explain why I am taking us in a slightly unconventional direction in looking at our lessons. As we look at texts filled with false prophets, corrupt priests, scribes, Pharisees, and sundry other biblical bad guys, I want to offer a homily in praise of hypocrisy.

We all know what a hypocrite is. A hypocrite is someone who says they hardly ever watch television and when they do it's only PBS, but on Sunday night they're not watching *Masterpiece Theatre*, they're watching *Breaking Bad* or *The Walking Dead* like the rest of us. Hypocrite is a wonderfully Greek word (*hupocritē*), its origin in Greek theater referring to one who performs before an audience or judge, so Greek it only occurs once in the Septuagint, the Greek translation of the Old Testament, Psalm 26:4, where the "hypocrites" are found in parallel with the "worthless." And this is something I'm going to praise? Stick with me.

If Paul had been born 700 years earlier he would have been Micah. Both were passionate in their faith, unfailing in their commitment, filled with equal parts spirit and vision. And both were fabulous fashioners of words, masters of rhetoric. It was Micah who gave us, "He has told you, O mortal, what is good; and what does the Lord require of you but to do justice, and to love kindness, and to walk humbly with your God?" (Mic 6:8), as fine a description of the life of faith as can be found in either testament. Paul, for all his bluster about weak and contemptible speech (2 Cor 10:10), was also a master of rhetoric, and could have held his own in a debate with Aristotle. While the target is slightly obscured in 1 Thessalonians by an elision in our lesson, it is fair to say that Micah and Paul are aiming in the same direction, at false prophets. Jesus was aiming at essentially the same target in his diatribe against the scribes and Pharisees.

Sometimes the lectionary reading omits a few verses, as in our epistle, and sometimes it stops just when things get interesting. Our Gospel reading is immediately followed by, "Woe to you, scribes and Pharisees, hypocrites!" a refrain found six times in this one chapter. The words are a curse, not in the sense of bad words you don't say in front of your mother, but as an invocation of divine judgment, the opposite of a blessing. So there you have it: Jesus cursed.

As long as we are talking about bad words this might be a good time to remind ourselves that "rhetoric" is not one of them. We usually think it is, as in, "Oh that's just a bunch of rhetoric." Many think the phrase "empty rhetoric" is an oxymoron. And then we complain that politicians today don't inspire us like Churchill, FDR, or JFK, and wish our preachers were better trained in the art of the homily.

Nobody complained about the quality of Jesus' preaching, although they did wonder where a carpenter's son found such skill. His artfully shaped parables, aphorisms, and sayings, his besting of opponents in debate, and the indelible impression of his teaching evidence both inspiration and craft. And when the occasion called for it, he knew how to dial up the rhetoric. Such is the case today, in a lesson from the last days before his Passion, as he offers a stinging rebuke of his most determined opponents. Jesus holds nothing back, going on in Matthew 23 to call them much worse than hypocrites—white-washed graves, blind guides, brood of vipers, greedy murderers. And those are the things Matthew could print.

Jesus focuses on the behavior, not the teachings, of the scribes and Pharisees, in no small measure because their teachings were not radically different from his own. In today's lesson the essential charge is that they do not practice what they preach, love their fancy titles, flaunt their ritual attire, like to sit up front at worship, and enjoy basking in the admiration of their followers. My God, they sound like Episcopal clergy!

We need take care here, as with the other lessons, not to mistake what Jesus is saying for disinterested reportage. It is anything but. Rather it is a highly charged and carefully chosen rhetorical argument, using hyperbole, analogy, and metaphor to drive home a point. The point is straightforward —pay attention to the good teaching even when the teacher is not a person of his or her words. The rhetoric is dangerous, and we must be careful never to allow its sharpness to justify anti-Semitism, in Matthew 23 and also the three verses of 1 Thessalonians omitted in our lection.

Jesus denounces the scribes and Pharisees as hypocrites. So how can I presume to praise hypocrisy? If a hypocrite is someone who says one thing but does another, how could I possibly suggest we give hypocrisy a second chance? Because the alternative to hypocrisy may well be worse.

How do you avoid being called a hypocrite? I can think of two ways. First, you could try being perfect. I know I've only been here a few months and don't know you that well, so don't take this personally, but I'm guessing perfect, you're not. So you can avoid hypocrisy by doing what most people do—refuse to stand for anything, never claim to believe something, and steadfastly avoid making a firm commitment. That way you will never be accused of not living up to your ideals. If you never preach you can't be guilty of not practicing.

What the world needs now is more hypocrites. Too many of us, too often, make lofty speeches about not wanting to be hypocrites. I'm not buying it. It's a dodge, a lame attempt not to be held accountable by claiming not to make a claim, take a stand, or confess a faith. I'm a realist here. You are likely as far from perfect as I am, so the temptation to avoid hypocrisy by hiding behind indecision, non-commitment, and taking all sides into account is real. But remember, temptation is something to resist.

Especially today, Stewardship Commitment Sunday. We are gathering the pledges, signing our commitments, reaffirming our place in this place. It is not a day for half-hearted I-don't-knows. It is a day for hypocrites. Lots of them. Big time. To be candid, we don't know what next year will bring, how the search process for a new dean will go, whether participation and membership in the cathedral will grow or slide. So what should we do? The prudent thing to do would be to stand pat, maybe scale back. But why be prudent? Go ahead and risk hypocrisy! Increase your pledge, offer your time in helpful service, call up the person you used to sit next to but haven't seen in a while, invite a friend to visit next Sunday. Sure, you might not be able to meet the financial challenge you set for yourself, the service you perform may not always feel rewarding, the parishioner you call could hang up on you, and your friend might not like the place. Big deal. The uncommitted can always find an excuse. The hypocrite rushes in and gives it a try!

Okay, maybe the praise of hypocrisy is bit much. But there are worse things to be called than a hypocrite. Better to try and not succeed, better to take a stand and stumble, than to passively watch the world go by in the name of not wanting to be a hypocrite. Do you know what you believe in, what matters most to you, what you feel God wants for you and of you? Good. Do others know? Even better. Does it mean you risk being called a hypocrite when you fail to live up to what you believe in? Sure, but that beats slip-sliding through life without an identity, without commitment, and without faith, even when you can't live up to the faith you profess and someone calls you a hypocrite.

Jesus, Micah, and Paul took courageous, unyielding stands for their faith, denouncing injustice and oppression, demanding integrity and righteousness. Only one of them was perfect.

Bibliography

Aristotle. *The Art of Rhetoric.* Translated by J. H. Freese. Loeb Classical Library 22. Cambridge, MA: Harvard University Press, 1932.

Bell, Rob. *Love Wins: A Book about Heaven, Hell, and the Fate of Every Person Who Ever Lived.* New York: Harper One, 2011.

Borg, Marcus J., and John Dominic Crossan. *The Last Week: The Day-by-Day Account of Jesus' Final Week in Jerusalem.* San Francisco: HarperOne, 2006.

Brosend, William. *Conversations with Scripture: The Parables.* Harrisburg, PA: Morehouse, 2006.

———. "The Feast of the Transfiguration." In *Feasts, Fasts and Holy Days,* edited by David Lott, 161. Philadelphia: Fortress, 2007.

———. *The Letters of James and Jude.* New Cambridge Bible Commentary. Cambridge: Cambridge University Press, 2004.

———. *The Preaching of Jesus: Gospel Proclamation Then and Now.* Louisville, KY: Westminster John Knox, 2010.

Buechner, Frederick. *Telling the Truth: The Gospel as Tragedy, Comedy and Fairy Tale.* San Francisco: Harper & Row, 1977.

Buttrick, David. *Homiletic: Moves and Structures.* Philadelphia: Fortress, 1987.

Church Publishing. *Book of Common Prayer.* New York: Church Publishing, 2011.

Covey, Stephen R. *The Seven Habits of Highly Effective People: Powerful Lessons in Personal Change.* New York: Simon & Schuster, 2013.

Craddock, Fred B. *As One without Authority.* Nashville: Abingdon, 1971.

———. *Overhearing the Gospel.* Nashville: Abingdon, 1978.

———. *Preaching.* Nashville: Abingdon, 1985.

Dykstra, Craig. "Pastoral and Ecclesial Imagination." In *For Life Abundant: Practical Theology, Theological Education, and Christian Ministry,* edited by Dorothy C. Bass and Craig Dykstra, 41–61. Grand Rapids: Eerdmans, 2008.

Fosdick, Harry Emerson. "What Is the Matter with Preaching?" *Harper's Magazine* 157 (1928) 133–41.

Hanh, Thich Nhat. *Peace is Every Step.* New York: Bantam, 1991.

Hiers, Sharon. "Peer Mentoring for Preachers: Helping Priests Become Better Preachers." DMin diss., University of the South, 2015.

Hipps, Shane. *Flickering Pixels.* Grand Rapids: Zondervan, 2009.

Hooker, Richard. *Of the Laws of Ecclesiastical Polity.* 2 vols. Eugene, OR: Wipf and Stock, 2013.

Lamott, Anne. *Bird by Bird: Some Instructions on Writing and Life.* New York: Anchor, 1994.

BIBLIOGRAPHY

Long, Thomas G. *The Witness of Preaching*. Louisville: Westminster John Knox, 2005.

McCarthy, Cormac. *The Crossing*. New York: Vintage, 1995.

Nouwen, Henri. *In the Name of Jesus: Reflections on Christian Leadership*. New York: Crossroad, 1989.

Proctor, Samuel D. *The Certain Sound of the Trumpet: Crafting a Sermon of Authority*. Valley Forge, PA: Judson, 1994.

Smith, Ted A., "Eschatological Memories of Everyday Life." In Charles Marsh, et al., *Lived Theology: New Perspectives on Method, Style, and Pedagogy*, 23–43. New York: Oxford University Press, 2016.

Teresa of Avila, *The Book of Her Life*. Collected Works 1. Translated by Kieran Kavanaugh and Otilio Rodriquez. Washington, DC: Institute of Carmelite Studies, 1987.

Taylor, Barbara Brown. *The Preaching Life*. Lanham, MD: Cowley, 1993.

Tisdale, Sallie. "The One in Front of You: A Consideration of Charity." *Harper's Magazine* 325 (2012) 45–52.

Troeger, Thomas H., and H. Edward Everding. *So That All Might Know: Preaching that Engages the Whole Congregation*. Nashville: Abingdon, 2008.